British Beginnings in WESTERN INDIA 1579-1657

British Beginnings in
WESTERN INDIA
1579-1657

An account of the early days of the British Factory of surat

H. G. RAWLINSON, M. A.

GYAN

Published by

Gyan Publishing House
5, Ansari Road
Daryaganj, New Delhi-110002
Phone: 011-47034999, 9811692060
E-mail: books@gyanbooks.com

Distribution Network
gyanbooks.com
India, USA, Canada, UK, Australia, France

ISBN: 978-81-212-8756-2 (PB)
First Published, 1920

2nd Impression 2023

Printed at: Gyan Press, Delhi.

BRITISH BEGINNIGS IN WESTERN INDIA 1579-1657
Author: H. G. Rawlinson

British Beginnings in
WESTERN INDIA

SURAT FORT FRONT VIEW

British Beginnings in WESTERN INDIA 1579–1657

An account of the early days of the British Factory of Surat

By

H. G. RAWLINSON, M.A.

INDIAN EDUCATIONAL SERVICE

OXFORD

At the CLARENDON PRESS

MCMXX

AUTHOR'S NOTE

My thanks are due to the Superintendent, Archaeological Survey, Western Circle, and to Mr. G. L. Steele, for the photographs of Surat which illustrate this book. The Committee of the Bhandarkar Oriental Research Institute, Poona, has permitted me to reproduce some of the matter in Chapter III, originally contributed to the *Bhandarkar Commemoration Volume* (1917). The late Dr. Vincent A. Smith not only read through the manuscript of this essay, but was good enough to revise the proofs, and to make many valuable corrections and suggestions. It was one of the last tasks of his life, and the author wishes to record his gratitude for the infinite pains which Mr. Smith took to help students of Indian history, and the ungrudging manner in which he devoted his time and energies to the service of others.

H. G. Rawlinson.

Dharwar,
February 1920.

CONTENTS

ILLUSTRATIONS

INTRODUCTION

For the majority of students, the history of British India virtually begins with Clive. Even those who possess a tolerable acquaintance with the last century of the Company's existence, often have a very hazy notion of the early struggles which preceded its triumphant establishment upon the throne of the Great Moghal. Yet this is a story of more than common interest, and the names of Best and Downton, Aldworth and Kerridge, and the other sturdy merchants and seamen, who, almost single-handed, carried on an unequal contest for so long against the attacks and plots of the Portuguese, and what was far more deadly, the onslaughts of disease and famine, deserve fuller recognition than they have hitherto received.

The English factory at Surat has been called the corner-stone of the British Empire in India. It was started as an experiment, at a time when every one thought that the real future of British enterprise in the East lay in the spice-trade of the Moluccas. At first the difficulties which stood in the way seemed almost insuperable. The Portuguese were furious at the violation of their alleged exclusive rights, guaranteed by a Papal Bull, to exploit the Orient. They not only opposed the intruders by sea, but placed every obstacle in their way upon land. At the Court at Agra, the astute Jesuits employed all sorts of devices to keep their hated rivals from gaining a footing. As for other difficulties, we have only to remember that the life of a man in Bombay was reckoned at 'two monsoons', and to note for ourselves the heavy toll which disease took upon such of the factors as enter into the history of the period, in order to realize how severe the struggle must have been. Added to this, we have to bear in mind that the voyage was a long and dangerous one. The annual 'fleet' dispatched by the Company arrived at uncertain intervals; and in the meantime, the factors were cut off from their friends, and isolated in a strange and hostile country without prospect of succour.

It has been said that *Robinson Crusoe* is a typically English novel. Crusoe is no hero. There is nothing romantic about him. He is just an ordinary British seaman, who, stranded on a distant shore, proceeds to make the best of the situation. In the same way, there is nothing romantic about the sturdy merchants who founded the factory at Surat. They were not consciously empire-builders. They did not come, like the Portuguese, with drum and trumpet to convert the East to the True Faith. They had no Camoens to sing their praises. They were not even supported, like the Dutch, by the State, from which, indeed, they received scant encouragement. They combined, in Puritan fashion, piety and profit; their objects were the glory of God, and the advancement of the Company's (and, incidentally, their own) interests. But they built better than they knew; and the footing which they established in Western India led to results far greater than they foresaw. The East India Company was one of the many companies which were the typically English means by which the Empire was built up. As Bacon says, 'trading in Companies is most agreeable to the English nature, which wanteth the same general vein of a Republic which runneth in the Dutch and serveth them instead of a Company'.

The history of Surat, the original head-quarters of the Company in Western India, is not a long one. The importance of the factory, at first the centre from which the whole of the Company's operations in the East were controlled, faded gradually before the rising star of Bombay. Surat had many disadvantages: by sea it was crippled by the lack of a good harbour, and by land it was open to incursions on the part of the Marathas. Hence Surat was destined never to become the capital of Western India. To-day it is a mere shadow of its former greatness: Swally Road is deserted, the ancient factory is a private dwelling-house, and the old walls and the quaint, crumbling tombs of the English and Dutch Presidents are the only monuments of its distinguished past.

The first person to make a systematic collection of the records and papers of the early adventurers in the East was Master Richard Hakluyt, who was set by Mr. Secretary

Walsingham to 'make diligent inquirie of such things as might yield any light unto our westerne discoverie in America'. Hakluyt extended his researches to cover English maritime enterprise in all directions. His monumental work, *The*

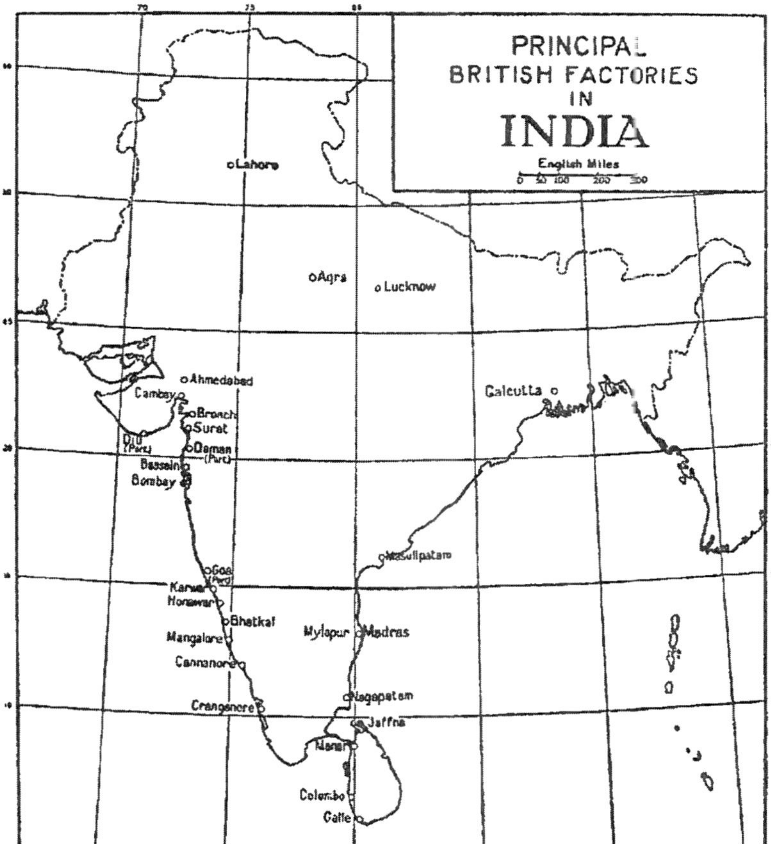

Principal Navigations, Voyages, Traffiques and Discoveries of the English Nation (1598–1600),[1] has been entitled 'the prose epic of the modern English nation'. It does not, however, deal with the history of the East India Company: this was left to Hakluyt's successor, Samuel Purchas, who took over

[1] Standard edition by MacLehose, Glasgow, 1903.

a number of his predecessor's manuscripts, and added material supplied by Sir Thomas Smythe, the Governor of the Company. His first publication was a summary, in the author's own words, entitled *Purchas his Pilgrimage, or Relation of the World and the Religions observed in all Ages*, of which four editions appeared between 1613 and 1626.[1] The last, considerably enlarged, formed a kind of appendix to his larger work, *Hakluytus Posthumus; or Purchas his Pilgrimes, containing a History of the World in Sea Voyages and Land Travels by Englishmen and Others.*[2] This volume is a compilation consisting of extracts from the journals of the voyagers themselves. Unfortunately, the material was so unwieldy that selection was necessary. Thus in one place the editor notes, 'This journal of Captain Keeling's and that of Captain Hawkins, very voluminous in a hundred sheets of paper, I have been bold so to shorten as to express only the most necessary observations for sea and land affairs'. For this Purchas has been severely but hardly fairly blamed. The standard of historical accuracy was not always what it is now. Much later,[3] we find the editor of Churchill's *Voyages* (said to be none other than John Locke) wishing that Hakluyt 'had been less voluminous, delivering what was really authentic and useful, and not stuffing his work with . . . so many warlike exploits not at all pertinent to his undertaking, and such a multitude of articles, charters, privileges, letters, relations, and other things little to the purpose of travels and discoveries'. Unfortunately we are able to supplement Purchas's extracts only in a few instances by reference to the originals. These precious documents have been in many cases destroyed, and in others left to rot. This would appear incredible, had we not the best testimony for this melancholy fact. 'Since 1836', writes Sir Clements Markham in his *Memoir on the Indian Surveys*,[4] 'all geographical and kindred subjects had been deprived of separate departmental super-

[1] The 1626 edition was reprinted by Talboys Wheeler in his *Early Travels in India*, First Series, Calcutta, 1864.

[2] Reprinted by MacLehose, Glasgow, 1905–7, 20 vols. References to 'Purchas' in the following pages refer to this edition.

[3] 1732.

[4] London, 1871, p. 284.

vision, and the maps, journals and other records had been cast aside to rot and perish. Those which were not lost were frayed and dust-stained, and finally a quantity were sold as waste-paper. Ancient journals of great navigators, abstracts of which alone exist in the *Pilgrims* of Purchas, have disappeared.' An instance of the vandalism which took place even in recent times is the disappearance, since 1849, of a page of Keeling's diary containing a reference to acting Shakespeare's plays on board ship.[1] Fortunately, a number of these relics have been now recovered and edited by members of the Hakluyt Society. Among the more important may be mentioned the journals of Hawkins, Jourdain, Keeling, and Sir Thomas Roe.

To the same society we are also indebted for a number of valuable editions of the works of contemporary travellers who visited Western India during the period, and left records of their impressions and experiences. Among these may be mentioned Huyghen van Linschoten, Pyrard de Laval, Pietro della Valle, Peter Mundy, and Fryer. Much, however, still remains to be done in this direction. The important works of Terry, Herbert, Lord, Ovington, Mandelslo, and Alexander Hamilton are still awaiting reprint, and can only be consulted in rare early editions. Mr. J. H. Ryley's *Ralph Fitch, England's Pioneer to India and Burma* (1899) is a useful compilation for the history of the first expedition to India; and Mr. E. F. Oaten's *European Travellers in India* (1909) gives a good outline and bibliography of the subject as a whole.[2]

The last and most valuable source of information, however, is to be found in the MS. records of the Company preserved at the India Office. These, unlike the mariners' journals, are official documents and are generally well preserved. They may be classified as (i) Original Correspondence (letters received by the Company from its servants in the East); (ii) Letter Books (office copies of letters dispatched by the

[1] Rundall, *Early Voyages to the North-West* (Hakluyt Society, p. 231). See p. 40, note 5, *infra*.

[2] Yule's *Hedges' Diary* is also a mine of miscellaneous information, much of which is valuable for the present purpose.

Company to its factories abroad); (iii) Factory Records (copies of letters dispatched and received, for each factory); and (iv) Court Minutes, containing the minutes of the Company's meetings. These are described in general terms in the late Sir George Birdwood's *Report on the Miscellaneous Records of the India Office* (1879). From time to time, series of letters and papers have been calendared and published; the following is a list of those which have appeared up to the present:

1. Calendar of State Papers, East Indies, China and Japan, 1513–1616. Ed. W. N. Sainsbury, 1862.
2. Calendar of State Papers, East Indies, China and Persia, 1625–9. Ed. W. N. Sainsbury, 1884.
3. Calendar of State Papers, East Indies, China and Persia, 1630–4. Ed. W. N. Sainsbury, 1892.
4. First Letter Book of the East India Company, 1600–19. Birdwood and Foster, 1893.
5. Dawn of British Trade to the East Indies as recorded in the Court Minutes of the East India Company, 1599–1613. H. Stevens, 1886.
6. Selections from the Letters, Despatches, and other State Papers, preserved in the Bombay Secretariat. G. W. Forrest, Bombay, 1885.
7. Letters received by the East India Company from its Servants in the East, 1602–7 (6 vols.). W. Foster and E. B. Sainsbury.
8. The English Factories in India, a Calendar of Documents in the India Office, 1618–55 (9 vols.). W. Foster and E. B. Sainsbury.
9. Court Minutes of the East India Company, 1635–59 (5 vols.). W. Foster and E. B. Sainsbury.

Of early histories of the Company, Macpherson's *History of the European Commerce with India* (1812) is of some value for one aspect of the subject. Bruce's book, *Annals of the East India Company*, 1600–1708, is the official account by the Company's historiographer. Neither Orme nor Mill contains any original matter of importance for the present purpose. The Rev. Philip Anderson's *English in Western*

India (Bombay, 1854) traverses the same ground as the present volume. It is an entertaining sketch, but it was written without consulting the India Office records, and is full of blunders which destroy its historical value. Sir William Hunter's *History of British India* (2 vols., 1899–1900) was left unfinished at the author's death: it contains valuable information, not always accurate, about the early history of the Company, but little to the purpose on Western India. Mr. Arnold Wright's *Early English Adventures in the East* appeared after the following pages had been penned.

CHAPTER I

THE QUEST AND INVENTION OF THE INDIES

FROM the days of Solomon to the end of the Middle Ages, trade between India and the West mainly followed the three great waterways of the Oxus, the Euphrates, and the Red Sea. The existence of a fourth route, round Africa, had indeed long been suspected. Herodotus[1] speaks of two attempts to circumnavigate Africa. Pharaoh Necho sent an expedition consisting of Phoenician mariners, who sailed down the Red Sea, and after three years returned through the Strait of Gibraltar. Xerxes permitted a Persian noble named Sataspes, who was lying under sentence of death, to expiate his crime by a similar feat. He set out in the opposite direction, through the Strait of Gibraltar, but returned after reaching a point called Soloeis, the modern Cape Spartel. Hanno the Carthaginian is also said to have gone as far as a place called Hesperi Cornu, perhaps the Bight of Benin.[2] Lastly, Eudoxus of Cyzicus, returning from a voyage to India made under the orders of Ptolemy Euergetes, about 120 B. C., was carried by stress of weather to the east coast of Africa. There he picked up the prow of a ship, which his sailors, judging by its appearance, declared to have come from Spain. Eudoxus was so impressed that on his return he fitted out an expedition of his own to circumnavigate Africa, but he was never heard of again.[3] The truth was, however, that a way round Africa to India was unnecessary while the infinitely nearer routes by way of Asia Minor were available, and the subject attracted little attention.

But the whole complexion of affairs was changed when the Turks conquered Constantinople in A. D. 1453. The trade-routes were now in the hands of a hostile power. The Genoese and Venetian factories in the Bosphorus were overwhelmed.

[1] Book iv, ch. 42–3.
[2] See his *Periplus* in C. Muller, *Geog. Graec. Minores*, vol. i.
[3] Strabo, *Geog.* ii. 3. 4.

Shipping lay rotting at the quays of Venice. The great European marts like Antwerp were crying out for spices. A new way to the East had to be discovered at all costs, and adventurous spirits set out to find one, across the Atlantic, round Africa, or through the Arctic ice-floes to the north-west or north-east.

Hakluyt rightly considers that the real value of the early explorers lies not so much in their actual achievements as in the information which they collected for the Portuguese in later days.

'Hath not Herodotus', he writes in his Preface, '(a man for his time most skilful and judicial in Cosmography, who writ above 2,000 years ago), in his 4th book called Melpomene, signified unto the Portugales in plain terms that Africa, except the small isthmus between the Arabian Gulf and the Mediterranean Sea, was on all sides environed with ocean? Sithens therefore these two worthy nations had those bright lamps of learning (I mean the most ancient and best philosophers, historiographers and geographers) to shew them light, and the loadstone of experience (to wit, those great exploits and voyages laid up in store and recorded) whereby to shape their course, what great attempt might they not presume to undertake?'

To us, the works of Strabo, Pliny, Arrian, and the other ancient geographers have now merely an academic interest, and we are apt to forget how anxiously they were scanned by the old discoverers from Venice, Genoa, Spain, and Portugal for any gleam of light which they might shed upon the secrets of the unexplored world.

The discovery of the new way to the East eventually fell to the lot of Portugal, and how this happened cannot better be told than in the quaint words of Purchas:[1]

'The loadstone was the lead-stone, the very seed and engendering stone of discovery, whosesoever jovial brain first conceived that Minerva. But the Juno Lucina that helped Nature in that happy conception and educated discovery to that strength that it durst ordinarily adventure beyond the known world, and made way to that maturity, whereby it opened soon after another World, was Prince Henry of Portugal.

[1] *Pilgrimes*, MacLehose's ed., Glasgow, 1905, ii. 1–18.

'Thus doth the great God raise up the least things to greatness; and this, one of the last and least of European kingdoms, was dignified with the first search and science of discovery. Spain and Portugal, after a long servitude, fattened their soil with the blood of the Moors, and thence have grown by Divine Blessing, not only to free themselves of that yoke, but with far-spreading boughs to overlook and overawe the remotest East and furthest West; paying themselves with the drugs and gems of Asia, the gold and slaves of Africa, silver and possessions of America, as wages for that European slavery under the Mahommedans, many ages continued.'

Prince Henry, as Purchas is careful to remind us, was half English, for his mother, the wife of John I, was Philippa, daughter of John of Gaunt. His original object was not the discovery of India so much as to institute a new crusade against the Mohammedans by carrying the war into their own country. As successive adventurers pushed farther and farther ahead, new vistas ever opened before their eyes; but the original idea remained, and to the end, the history of Portuguese dominion in India is the history of the last great crusade against the infidel. Herein lay the secret of their weakness and their strength.

'The illustrious Henry', Purchas continues, 'having given proof of his valour against the Infidels at Cepta, devised with himself how he (being Governor of the Military Order of Jesus Christ, formerly instituted and endowed to maintain wars against the Moors, now already expelled out of Portugal) might advance the honour of his Name and Order in conquests which others had not yet attempted, and therefore in discoveries of Countries yet unknown. To this end he spent his life in single estate and in the studies of the Mathematics; for which purpose he chose the clearer air of Cape S. Vincent, that there he might better intend his mathematical theory, the practike thereof in instruments, and the use in sending out ships at his own charge to discover remoter parts, whereof he had both heard by enquiry of captives taken at Cepta and conceived by his own study and reason, that the Atlantic and Indian Seas had concourse, the one yielding passage to the other, or rather being one continued ocean.'

The heroic work went on slowly and painfully.

'Twelve years had passed, since the Prince had begun this enterprise, before Cape Bajadore could be passed, such was the conceit of tempestuous seas, strong currents, whirlpools which could swallow ships, beyond that Cape. . . . But the Prince never gave over his endeavours of discovery till he discovered the Celestial Jerusalem, which happened the thirteenth of November 1463, three and forty years after Madeira had been descried; in all which time his travel succeeded no further than from Bajadore to Sierra Liona, one thousand one hundred and ten miles space in near fifty years continued discovery. *So hard a thing is it to discover.*'

The Prince was dead, but his spirit lived in the breasts of his countrymen. They crept ever farther and farther down the coast, erecting crosses, converting the natives, or kidnapping them for slaves, and seeking for the kingdom of the legendary Prester John, until, in 1487, Bartholomew Diaz 'first discovered the famous Cape which for his manifold troubles he termed Cabo Tormentoso, or the tempestuous Cape; but King John, hoping thence to discover the Indies, named it at his return the Cape of Good Hope'. At the same time, one Peter Covilian, travelling via Constantinople and Aden, had actually managed to reach Goa and Calicut. On his return he was detained at the Abyssinian court, but he managed to send back to his master a map of the coast of East Africa and the way to India. Armed with Covilian's map, Vasco Da Gama, after many anxious months of training, and the utmost care in the selection of tackle, stores, medicines, and charts, sailed in splendid pomp from Lisbon, with three ships and 160 men, on July 9, 1497. On May 20, 1498, he cast anchor off Calicut, and the Cape route to India was opened.

Meanwhile, other great discoveries had been made in the West. Christopher Columbus, a Genoese, had offered his services to Portugal for the discovery of a western route to India, but finding himself neglected, had transferred himself to Spain, with the result that Spain became the mistress of America. The discovery of America caused much anxiety in Portugal, as it was believed that the West Indies were actually the outworks of the Asiatic continent, and that Spain had found a short cut to India. The matter was referred to the Vatican, which as long ago as 1441 had granted to Prince Henry 'a perpetual donation to the Crown of Portugal of whatsoever should be discovered from Cape Bajadore to the East Indies exclusively '.[1] Alexander VI thereupon issued his famous Bull of 1493,[2] by which he sought to indicate the precise limit of the Spanish claims. Addressing ' Our dearly beloved Son in Christ, King Ferdinand, and to our deare beloved daughter in Christ Elizabeth, Queen of Castile ', he ordained that:

> ' By the fullness of Apostolical power, we do give, grant and assign to you, your heirs and successors, all the firm land and islands, found or to be found, discovered or to be discovered, towards the West and South, drawing a line from the Pole Arctic to the Pole Antarctic, that is from the North to the South ; containing in this donation whatsoever firm lands or islands are found or to be found towards India or towards any other part, whatsoever it be, being distant from or without the aforesaid line drawn 100 leagues towards the West and South from any of the Islands which are commonly called De Los Azores and Capo Verde.'[3]

This settlement was not very definite, and complications arose from time to time. Pinçon, a Portuguese mariner, discovered Brazil, and claimed it for Portugal in 1499; on the other hand, Magellan in 1521 claimed the Philippines for Spain. After much discussion the boundary line was fixed in 1506 at 370 leagues west of Cape Verde,[4] but as Portugal found herself fully satisfied with her Indian possessions, while the plunder of the silver mines of Spain and Mexico satiated even Spanish rapacity, the matter finally adjusted itself. Portugal was to have the East Indies; Spain, the West Indies. Besides, with the intrusion of England on their sphere of operations, both sides gave up mutual rivalry in order to repulse the heretic. By the Convention of Saragossa (1529), Charles V sold his rights in the Moluccas, and the eastern boundary was fixed at 297 leagues to the east of those islands. The dispute finally ended when the Spanish and

[1] Purchas, *op. cit.*, ii. 14.

[2] For text, translation, and commentary, see Purchas, *op. cit.*, pp. 32–64. It was ' Englished ' for Purchas by R. Eden, 1577.

[3] According to the ideas of the time, the nation which discovered a trade-route had the exclusive right to use it. The English, in protesting by force of arms against this alleged right, were asserting the ' freedom of the seas ' to all comers.

[4] Treaty of Tordesillas, 1494–1506.

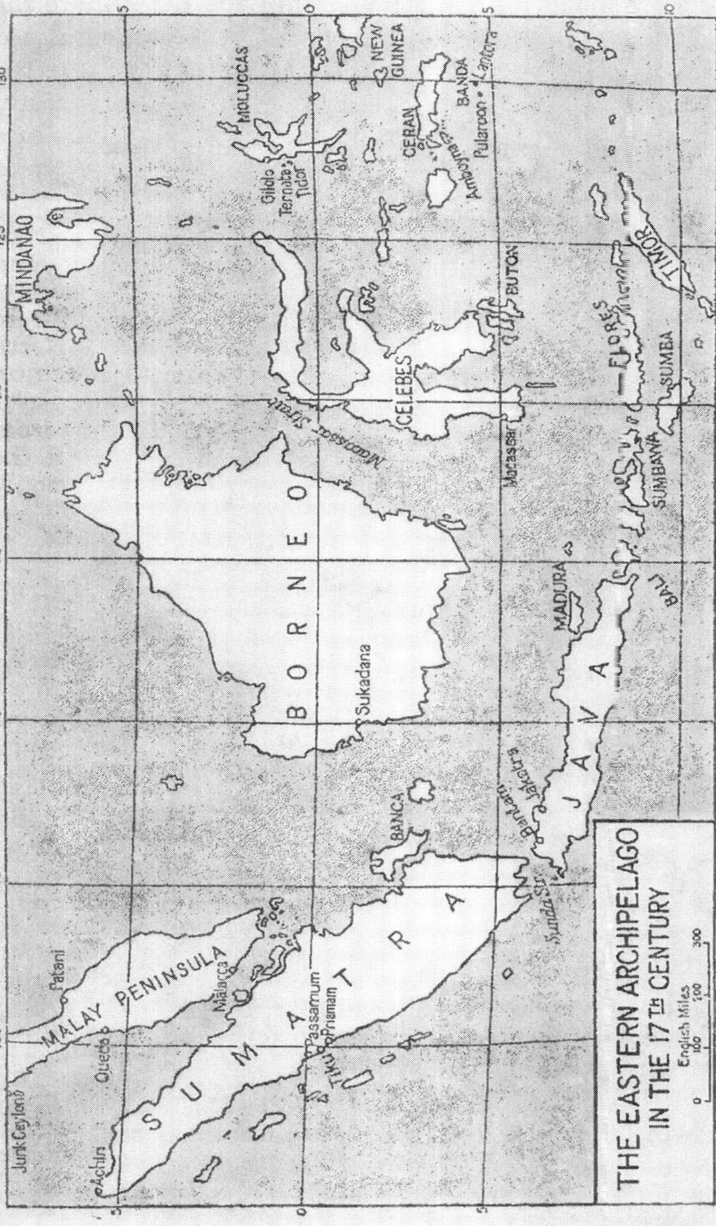
THE EASTERN ARCHIPELAGO
IN THE 17TH CENTURY
English Miles
0 100 200 300
MINDANAO
MOLUCCAS
Gilolo
Ternate
Tidor
NEW GUINEA
CERAN
BANDA
Amboyna
Pularoon
Lantore
BUTON
CELEBES
Macassar Strait
Macassar
FLORES
TIMOR
SUMBA
SUMBAWA
BALI
MADURA
B O R N E O
Sukadana
J A V A
Jakatra
Bantam
Sunda Str.
BANCA
S U M A T R A
MALAY PENINSULA
Patani
Malacca
Passamum
Priamam
Tiku
Queda
Junk Ceylon
Achin

Portuguese crowns were united in 1580, though this, as we shall see, proved fatal to the smaller kingdom. Purchas and other contemporary writers wax wroth at the Pope's presumption in thus partitioning the world. But there was nothing in the proceeding contrary to mediaeval notions of justice: the Pope was the recognized international authority previous to the Reformation, and besides, Portugal had professedly set out on her Eastern adventure as the servant of the Cross.

It is impossible here to give an account of the rise and growth of the Portuguese Empire in the East up to the time of the appearance of the English in India. Under Albuquerque (1509–15) her power reached its zenith. Albuquerque captured Goa in 1510. He conquered Ormuz in 1515, and by this means put the control of the Persian Gulf route in the hands of Portugal. He almost succeeded in seizing Aden, the key to the Red Sea, and actually occupied Socotra. Along the west coast of India a string of Portuguese forts stretched from Diu to Cochin, while on the east coast they held St. Thomé and Negapatam; in Ceylon, Manaar, Colombo, and Galle; in the Far East, Amboyna, Tidore, Macao, and Manilla; and on the coast of Africa, Sofala and Mozambique.

But by the end of the sixteenth century, when the English appeared upon the scene, they had already begun to decline. The primary cause of their fall was, of course, their failure to maintain their power on the sea. The union of the Spanish and Portuguese crowns involved the latter nation in the defeat of the Armada, and the fate of the Portuguese Empire in the East was decided by that encounter, just as later the fate of the French in India was settled by the Battle of the Nile.[1] But other causes were at work which made degeneration inevitable. There were no permanent elements in the great fabric erected by Da Gama and Albuquerque. The Portuguese came to India not as merchants or colonists, but as Crusaders. This led them to commit acts of cruelty which

[1] The fall of Vijayanagar (1565) also had a disastrous effect on their prosperity. Goa was, besides, a very unhealthy spot, and was devastated by periodical epidemics—cholera in 1543 (Fonseca, *Historical Sketch of Goa*, p. 146) and epidemic fever in 1570 and 1635 (*ibid.*, pp. 149, 169).

made them detested by the inhabitants of the country. Da Gama's followers thought nothing of stuffing an Arab merchant's mouth with dirt and fastening it up with a slice of pork, or cutting off the ears of a Brahmin spy and sewing dog's ears to his head. The massacre, mutilation, and torture of captives was the rule rather than the exception.[1] The horrors of the Inquisition were afterwards added to the brutalities of forcible conversion, and were applied even to the unoffending Nestorian Christians. Temples were plundered as a religious duty. The sacred Tooth of the Buddha, reverenced by millions in Ceylon, Burma, and Siam, was pounded in a mortar and hurled into the sea. It was only adverse winds which saved Albuquerque from attempting a raid upon Medina with the object of holding up the body of the Prophet to ransom in exchange for the Holy Sepulchre. It is difficult even to imagine the effect of such an enterprise upon the Moslem world. It is true that after 1570 the Portuguese secured the patronage of the Mughal court. But this was due to the unwearied diplomacy of the Jesuit Mission which settled at Agra in the time of Akbar, and maintained for the next fifty years an unceasing struggle against English attempts to procure a *farman* from the Emperor. The Moghals were too powerful and too distant to feel the effects of Portuguese fanaticism, or the results might have been very different. At Goa, and throughout Portuguese India, corruption and venality were widespread, for the Portuguese, too proud to earn money honestly by trade, were driven to make it by less honourable means.

'Society was almost rotten to the core', says one of their own countrymen. 'The morals of the community were extremely lax. Profligacy had become the predominant and fashionable vice, and men gave themselves up to the sensual pleasures peculiar to Oriental life Nor was the public administration less tainted. The civic virtues of Albuquerque

[1] Almeida did this at Diu (1509), while at Cannanore he blew his prisoners from his ships' guns. In 1507 an unoffending Arab crew was sewn up in sails and drowned. These are only isolated examples of common brutality. Albuquerque, from motives of policy, confined his cruelty to the Mohammedans and favoured the Hindus (Fonseca, *Historical Sketch of Goa*, p. 144), but his partial toleration was not followed by his successors.

and Castro were supplanted by corruption and venality; justice was bought, public offices were put up for sale, and the martial spirit degenerated into effeminacy, sloth, and indolence, as in the last days of the Roman Empire.'[1]

The same story is told by Linschoten, who speaks of the women as being secluded in semi-Oriental privacy, and indulging in intrigues before the very eyes of their husbands, whom they drugged with *datura*.[2]

One of the capital mistakes of the Portuguese was their attempt to found colonies in tropical countries. They seem to have been indifferent to the dangers of miscegenation. Albuquerque even encouraged it,[3] and this led to very rapid deterioration, physical and moral. 'The truth is', writes Parson Terry in 1616, 'that the Portuguese, especially those which are born in those Indian colonies, most of them a mix'd seed begotten upon those natives, are a very low, poor-spirited people, called therefore *Gallinas dell Mar*, the hens of the sea!'[4] At first sight, it appears paradoxical that Terry, who gives such a spirited account of the fight between his vessel and Don Emmanuel de Menzes, should speak in these terms of Portuguese gallantry. But Fryer, writing in 1681, confirms him. 'The Portugals,' he says, 'generally forgetting their pristine virtue, lust, riot and rapine, the ensuing consequences of a long undisturbed peace where wealth abounds, are the only remarkable reliques of their ancient worth; their courages being so much effeminated that it is a wonder to most how they keep anything, if it were not that they have lived among mean-spirited neighbours.'[5] Those gallant sailors, De Menzes, Ruy Frere, Bothelo, and the rest, who so strenuously resisted the progress of the English in India, came straight out from home, and their crews were stiffened with large European drafts, of very different mettle from the

[1] Quoted in Fonseca, *Historical Sketch of Goa*, p. 168. The whole of chapter vi of that work is devoted to an analysis of the causes of the decline and fall of Goa.

[2] See the note on this quoted from Pyrard (ii. 69) in Fonseca, p. 162.

[3] Albuquerque 'aimed at cementing the union of the rulers and the ruled. He therefore encouraged intermarriages between them, by loading the married pairs with substantial gifts' (Fonseca, p. 143).

[4] Terry, *Voyage* (1777 ed.), p. 153.

[5] *New Account*, ed. Crooke, Hakluyt Society, i. 165.

mestico, or Goanese half-caste. Pietro della Valle, himself a Catholic, who visited Goa in 1623, speaks sadly of the poverty which the Portuguese strove in vain to conceal. 'They live in outward appearance with splendour enough,' he notes, 'however in secret they endure many hardships, and some there are who, to avoid submitting to such employments as they judge unbecoming to their gravity, lead very wretched lives, undergoing much distress and being put to beg every day in the evening.'[1]

President Fremlin reports in a similar strain to the Company in 1640. 'They are undoubtedly in a most miserable predicament,' he writes, 'Malacca and Ceylon besieged, and, the Dutch say, as good as seized: their galleons fired: their soldiers decayed: themselves disheartened: and all precipitating them, except sudden and ample succours from Europe reinforce them, even to utter ruin, whilst the insolent Dutch domineer in all places, styling themselves already Kings of the Indian Seas.'[2]

The way, therefore, was open to England. The Dutch never cast their eyes seriously upon the Indian mainland. Their concern was with the Spice Islands, and after the Massacre of Amboyna, in 1623, the English withdrew from competition with them in that quarter, devoting themselves to the development of their factories in India. The English came to India in a very different spirit from the Portuguese. At first they sought neither colonies nor converts: they came neither as crusaders nor as conquerors, but as simple merchants. 'A war and traffic are incompatible', writes Roe to his employers. 'It is the beggaring of the Portuguese, notwithstanding his many rich residences and territories, that he keeps soldiers that spend it. He never profited by the Indies since he defended them.'[3] They were plain merchants, very different from the haughty hidalgos of Goa. They had little liking for the upper classes. The Company even requested the Crown 'to be allowed to sort their business

[1] *Travels*, ed. Gray (Hakluyt Society), i. 157.
[2] *English Factories in India*, 1637–41, p. 230.
[3] Roe, ed. Foster, p. 344.

with men of their own quality, lest the suspicion of the employment of *gentlemen*, being taken hold of by the generality, do drive a great number of the adventurers to withdraw their contributions'![1] But the sturdy adventurers of the reigns of Elizabeth and James I had other ambitions besides making money: they also meant to show the world, as Hawkins put it, that 'the King of England's licence is as good as the King of Spain's, and he that saith the contrary is a liar'. Then as now, our merchant-skippers were not out to fight, but they had no objection to defending themselves if molested when in pursuit of their calling. 'So carry yourself', run the instructions to a captain in the Muscovy Company, 'that God may be glorified, our country benefitted, yourself credited, and we in our desires satisfied.' We may smile at the quaint devices of our Puritan ancestors to uphold a high standard of morality in the Company's ships and factories—the frequent injunctions against 'brabbling', gambling, profanity, and drunkenness, the provision of chaplains and edifying literature, and rules enjoining daily prayers and a common table in the factory; but no doubt these measures did much to save us from the degeneracy which fell like a blight upon Goa. How strict, for instance, were the rules against *liaisons* with Indian women, may be gathered from the case of John Leachland. In 1625 it transpired that

> 'John Leachland having for some passed years privately kept a woman of this country and by her had a child. . . . And notwithstanding the many persuasions both of the President and Council to divert him from that course of life, standeth so firmly resolute not to leave her, as that he desireth rather to be suspended the Company's service.'[2]

President Wylde thereupon reported him to the Company, with the result that he was cashiered. He continued, however, to live in Surat with his native wife and his daughter Mary until he died in the great famine of 1630, whereupon the President took charge of Mary, educated her, and married her, with a small dowry, to an English tailor employed at

[1] Quoted in Mill, *History of India* (1826 ed.), i. 123.
[2] *Factory Records*, Surat, i. 117.

the factory.[1] This, of course, cannot have been an isolated case, for Englishwomen were not allowed in the early days of the Company to come to India, except by special permission; but the action of the authorities shows how strong was the feeling on this subject, and we are able to understand why Surat was not, like Goa, overrun with degenerate half-castes.

We have remarked that the East India Company was founded and supported by the Puritan mercantile class, the inveterate enemies of the Catholic powers. The greatest of the Puritans, sitting in solitude and meditating, 'by dangers and with darkness compassed round', upon his vast epic, while his countrymen, sunk in sloth and luxury, allowed Dutch guns to thunder at their gates, often turned to the Eastern ventures of the associates of his youth for his most striking similes. Instances are innumerable, but few readers of *Paradise Lost* can have forgotten the beautiful comparison of the flying Fiend to a fleet,

By equinoctial winds
Close sailing from Bengala or the isles
Of Ternate and Tidore, whence merchants bring
Their spicy drugs;

or the vision of Adam, where he sees

the destined walls
Of Cambalu, seat of Cathaian Can,
And Samarchand by Oxus, Temir's throne,
To Paquin of Sinaean kings, and thence
To Agra and Lahore of Great Mogul
Down to the Golden Chersonese . . .
Mombaza, and Quiloa, and Melind,
And Sofala thought Ophir;

or the graphic picture of

The utmost Indian isle Taprobané,
Dusk faces with white silken turbants wreathed;

or the banyan tree, which

In Malabar or Deccan spreads her boughs
High over-arched, with echoing walks between.

[1] Peter Mundy, *Travels* (Hakluyt Society), ed. Temple, ii. 354.

And lastly, when we read how

> High on a throne of royal state, which far
> Outshone the wealth of Ormuz and of Ind
> Or where the gorgeous East with richest hand
> Showers on her kings barbaric pearl and gold,
> Satan exalted sat,

we can see that the poet's mind has gone back to Sir Thomas Roe's famous description of his first interview with Jahangir, when 'high in a gallery, with a canopy over him and a carpet before him, sat in great and barbarous state the Great Mogul'.

CHAPTER II

THE FIRST ENGLISHMEN IN INDIA

According to the Anglo-Saxon Chronicle, the first Englishman to visit India was one Sighelm in A. D. 883. He was sent by King Alfred on a pilgrimage 'to India, to Saint Thomas and Saint Bartholomew', words which are interpreted as referring to the famous shrine of St. Thomas, the Apostle of India, at Mylapore (Mailapur). This was in fulfilment of a vow made by the king when London was besieged by the Danes in or about 880.[1] Florence of Worcester[2] calls the envoy Swithelm, and informs us that he was Bishop of Sherborne. William of Malmesbury,[3] who calls him Sigelinus, Bishop of Sherborne, says that he made the journey with great success, 'at which everybody in this age wonders', whence we infer that a journey to India appeared to be an almost incredible thing to an Englishman in the twelfth century. He adds that he brought back what Hakluyt picturesquely calls 'many strange and precious unions [pearls] and costly spices', which were still preserved in the latter's day, and 'yet extant in the muniments of the church'. Gibbon (chap. xlvii) unkindly suggests that Sighelinus went no farther than Egypt for his curios. The only other Englishman said to have visited India before Tudor days was the semi-mythical Sir John Mandeville. But his adventures, which include a visit to the Well of Youth at Polombe (Quilon on the Malabar coast), are mostly an ingenious farrago of the works of Friar Odoric, Hetoum the Armenian, Carpini, and others. It is beyond reasonable doubt that the book was compiled by a certain physician

[1] *Anglo-Saxon Chronicle*, ed. and transl. Thorpe, 1861, i. 150 and ii. 66.

[2] d. A. D. 1117.

[3] *Gesta Regum Anglorum*, etc., ed. Hardy, 1840, i. 187: 'Elfredus . . . trans mare Romam, et ad sanctum Thomam in India, multa munera misit. Legatus in hoc missus Sigelinus, Scireburnensis episcopus, cum magna prosperitate, quod quivis hoc seculo miretur, Indiam penetravit; inde rediens, exoticos splendores gemmarum, et liquores aromatum, quorum illa humus ferax est, reportavit' (*c.* A. D. 1120). See Bishop Medlycott, *India and the Apostle Thomas* (Nutt, 1905).

of Liège. The travels are alleged to have extended from 1322 to 1355.[1]

England was early stirred to take part in the new world opened out by the discoveries of Spain and Portugal.

'The Indes are discovered', runs a petition addressed to Henry VIII in 1511,[2] 'and vast treasure brought from thence every day. Let us therefore bend our endeavours thitherwards; and if the Spaniards and Portuguese suffer us not to join with them, there will be yet region enough for all to enjoy.'

At first, however, England, bound by the Pope's award, had to confine her efforts to attempts to discover a north-west or north-east passage to India through the Arctic Ocean. Even after the Reformation many gallant lives were thrown away over this will-o'-the-wisp, for it was not until Drake in 1578 penetrated into the Southern Ocean, and called at Tidore in the heart of the Spice Islands on his homeward voyage, that the spell was broken. Cavendish repeated the feat in 1586, and the defeat of the Spanish Armada two years later finally asserted England's supremacy over the Catholic powers by sea and laid the foundations of her overseas empire. Hakluyt, however, is anxious that we should not forget those gallant, albeit unsuccessful, pioneers, who cheerfully gave their lives for the cause.

'Be it granted', he writes, 'that the renowned Portugal, Vasques da Gama, traversed to main Ocean Southward of Africk: did not the valiant English knight Sir Hugh Willoughby: did not the famous pilots Stephen Borough, Arthur Pet, and Charles Jackman accoast Nova Zembla, Colgoieve, and Vaigatz to the north of Europe and Asia? Howbeit you will say, perhaps, not with the like golden success, not with such deductions of Colonies nor attaining of conquests. True it is that our success hath not be correspondent unto theirs: yet in this our attempt the uncertainty of finding was far greater and the difficulty and danger of searching no whit less. . . . For first they were to expose themselves unto the rigour of the stern and uncouth Northern seas and to make trial of the swelling waves and boistrous winds which there commonly do surge and blow: then were

[1] *Encyclopaedia Britannica*, 11th ed., *s.v.*
[2] Quoted in Macpherson, *Annals of Commerce* (1805 ed.), ii. 39.

they to sail by the ragged and perilous coast of Norway and to frequent the unchaunted shores of Finmark, to double the dreadful and misty North Cape, to bear with Willoughby's land, to run along within kenning of the countries of Lapland and Corelia, and as it were to open and unlock the sevenfold mouth of Dvina. Moreover in their Northeasterly navigations upon the seas and by the coasts of Condora, Colgoieve, Petzora, Joughoria, Samoedia, Nova Zembla, etc, and their passing and return through the Straits of Vaigats, unto what drifts of snow and mountains of ice they were subject and in danger of, I wish you rather to learn out of the voyages of Sir Hugh Willoughby, Stephen Borough, Arthur Pet and the rest, than to expect in this place an endless catalogue thereof.'

Meanwhile, certain Englishmen had already found their way to India. Their adventures are so remarkable, and the information which they collected was so valuable for stimulating further enterprise in this direction, that it will be necessary to narrate their adventures in detail. The honour of being the first Englishman to set foot in India (if we except Sighelm and Mandeville) belongs to Father Thomas Stevens, S.J.[1] Accounts of his early life are vague and conflicting, but apparently he was born at Bulstan in Wiltshire in 1549.[2] He appears to have been educated at Winchester.[3] He was brought up as a Catholic, and when the persecution of the Catholics became more and more bitter, he and his friend Thomas Pound resolved to flee to Rome. Pound was arrested, but Stevens escaped, and was enrolled as a novice at the Seminary of Santa Andrea in October 1575. His brother Richard, with whom he is often confused,[4] meanwhile went to New College, Oxford, where he apparently espoused Protestantism. Subsequently, however, he returned to the ancient faith and took high honours at Douai and Paris. At Rome, Thomas studied under Garnett and Parsons, and met Campion. He did not, however, return with these gallant

[1] The following details are mainly borrowed from the Introduction to the *Christian Purana* by J. L. Saldanha (Mangalore, 1907), and the notice in the *Dictionary of National Biography*, Supplement, vol. iii, p. 355. The name is also spelt Stephens. [2] Foley, *Records S. J.*, viii. 1453.

[3] Thomas Stevens, a native of Bourton, Dorset, was entered as a scholar of Winchester, aged 13, in 1564 (Kirby, *Winchester Scholars*, p. 139).

[4] Thus, when Hakluyt says *Thomas* graduated at Oxford in 1577, he must be referring to *Richard*.

men to meet death in his native land: a perusal of the works of St. Francis Xavier had filled him with dreams of the East, and he applied for permission to go as a missionary to Goa. He went to Lisbon, and sailed with a fleet of five ships bound for India on April 4, 1579. On his arrival he wrote a letter [1] to his father, dated November 10, 1579, which contains a long description of his adventures. As Stevens's father was a prominent London merchant, this epistle,[2] arriving at a time when all men's minds were intent upon India, aroused the greatest interest. It was passed from hand to hand, and in 1583 we find Master Newbery, who had borrowed it from Hakluyt to copy out, returning it to him from Aleppo.[3] The fleet, Stevens tells us, was late in starting, which caused them to miss the monsoon off Africa and nearly led to disaster. They sailed from Lisbon with much pomp, with bands playing and flags flying, but 'in the manner of war'. The precaution was necessary, for off Madeira, a daring English cruiser hove in sight, and dogged them all the way to the Canary Islands, not giving up the chase until the Portuguese 'laid out their greatest ordnance'. 'The English ship was very fair, which I was sorry to see so ill occupied', Stevens remarks, his sympathies divided between his religion and his country. The voyage was diversified by the usual excitements of flying fish and sharks, and in the absence of proper charts or astronomical instruments every bird and every change in the sea or atmosphere was anxiously scanned in order that they might ascertain the names of the countries which they passed. At the Cape of Good Hope, 'the point so famous and feared of all men', they nearly ran aground, but were saved by a change of the wind. It was now the end of July, and the captain, instead of putting in at Mozambique

[1] Given in Hakluyt, *Principal Navigations*, ed. MacLehose, vol. vi, pp. 377 ff.; also in Purchas.

[2] We should, however, guard against the statement made by the *Ency. Brit.* (10th ed.), xii. 798, and often repeated, that 'Stevens' *letters* are said to have aroused great enthusiasm in England to trade directly with India'. Only one such letter was known to Hakluyt. Thomas promises his father to 'write once again', but there is no evidence that he fulfilled the promise. The Portuguese may have prevented him.

[3] See *Ralph Fitch*, J. Horton Ryley, 1899, p. 207.

to rest for a month and refit, decided to head straight for India; but the pilot, misled by contrary gales and currents, eventually found himself off Socotra! Here, however, 'God sent great winds from the North East' (in other words, the monsoon had set in), and by October the 24th, they arrived off Goa, in sore straits for food and water, and with half the crew incapacitated by scurvy. Another letter, written by Stevens in Latin in 1583 to his brother in Paris, is chiefly interesting as throwing light upon missionary methods in those early days.[1] Stevens tells of a certain Peter Bruno, who burnt the temple at Cuncolim after slaying a cow upon the altar of the idol, and was torn to pieces by an enraged mob.[2] A young Brahmin convert was drugged with *datura* by his relations and smuggled away, only escaping after many adventures. Father Stevens, now admitted to priest's orders, was eventually (February 10, 1587–9) made spiritual coadjutor, Rector of Salsette College,[3] and minister of the *domus professorum* at Goa. For forty years he laboured among his flock, and while in Goa he was enabled to render signal service to his fellow-countrymen, Fitch, Newbery, and their friends, who were detained by the authorities, as will be subsequently narrated. Later on he did a similar kindness for the French traveller, Pyrard de Laval, and we also find him giving a letter of recommendation to Sir Thomas Shirley.[4] It is said that on his death-bed he admitted that the Portuguese were 'too suspectless in admitting foreigners', but the story is doubtful, in view of the well-known jealousy of the authorities.[5] Though wellnigh forgotten in England, the name of Padre Estevão, the Apostle of Salsette, is still venerated by the Christians of the Konkan, among whom

1 Reprinted by Saldanha from the original at Brussels Library.

2 In the same massacre perished the famous Father Rodolfo Aquaviva, the friend of Akbar (V. A. Smith, *Akbar*, p. 206) with three other priests, July 15, 1583. The 'Martyrs of Cuncolim' were beatified in 1893 (Fonseca, *Historical Sketch of Goa*, p. 47).

3 Described by Fonseca, p. 48.

4 *Calendar State Papers*, E. i, 1519–1616, no. 574.

5 The much-maligned Jesuits often helped their Protestant fellow-countrymen in the East. See e.g. Joseph Salbanke's narrative in Purchas, vol. iii. He was a prisoner in Muscat in 1608, and 'like to abide there for ever' until released by Father Drury, a Jesuit.

he worked till his death in 1619. This remarkable man has another claim upon our admiration. Not only was he the first Englishman to visit India, but he was the first and only Englishman to write a great poem in an Indian language.[1]

In his letter to his brother Richard referred to above he had spoken of his interest in the Indian languages, which, anticipating the discoveries of the philologists, he described as 'agreeable in pronunciation and in structure allied to Greek and Latin'. He afterwards produced a grammar in the Konkani or coast dialect of Marathi, and a catechism in Kanarese, the language of the western Karnatak, both of which were published after his death.[2] But his great work, published in 1615,[3] was the *Christian Purana*, an epic in the Konkani dialect of Marathi spoken by his flock, which deals, like Milton's more famous work, with

> Man's first disobedience, and the fruit
> Of that forbidden Tree, whose mortal taste
> Brought death into the world and all our woe.

The *Christian Purana*, however, covers a much wider field. Its subject is nothing less than a versified account of the whole Bible story, from the Creation to the foundation of the Church, including such episodes as the visit of Christ to Limbo and the Harrowing of Hell, which, though not found in the Scriptures, have the *imprimatur* of the Catholic religion.[4] It is a long work, comprising ninety-five cantos and eleven thousand *slokas* or couplets. One of the many remarkable features of the poem is the ingenious system of transliteration adopted, for, owing no doubt to the impossibility of printing at that date in any Indian script, Stevens was obliged to employ

[1] His only European rival is another Catholic missionary, Father Beschī, the Tamil poet.

[2] The works in the National Library, Lisbon, are: (1) *Doctrina Christā em Lingua Bramana-Canarin*, em Rachol, 1622; (2) *Arte da Lingua Canarin*, em Rachol, 1640; (3) *Discorso sobre a Vinda de Jesus Christo*, Goa, 1626, 1649, 1654.

[3] Subsequent editions appeared, but only manuscript copies have survived. It is said that the printed ones were all destroyed by Tipu Sultan.

[4] The author's idea, as he explains in the early part of the poem, was to replace by a *Christian* Purana, the heathen epics, Puranas, &c., of the Hindus, in the recitation of which the Indian people take a perennial delight.

Roman characters.[1] For the Marathi language the poet expresses great admiration.

> 'Like a jewel among pebbles', he sings in the *Purana*, 'like a sapphire among jewels, is the excellence of the Marathi tongue. Like the jasmine among blossoms, the musk among perfumes, the peacock among birds, the Zodiac among the stars, is Marathi among languages.'

It is an interesting fact that Stevens was a contemporary of the Marathi poet Eknath (1548–1609) and that both employ the *Ovi* metre. Hence Stevens may be fairly reckoned among the poets of the Marathi Renaissance which afterwards produced Tukaram and Ramdas, the great national singers of the Deccan in the age of Sivaji.

Father Stevens was only indirectly connected with British enterprise in India. But his famous letter largely influenced the merchants of London in their decision to send a band of picked adventurers to report upon the commercial possibilities of the East Indies. This expedition was 'chiefly set foorth' by Richard Staper and Sir Edward Osborne, then Lord Mayor of London.[2] These great merchants had taken a prominent part in the development of English overseas commerce. Staper had been on an embassy to Constantinople in 1579, and they had been associated with two other city merchants in the Levant Company of 1582. It was the Levant Company which established, in 1583, an English consul at Tripolis, and this in turn led to a further charter granted three years later to a company of traders whose chief mart was Aleppo, where also was an English consul. Apparently the original idea in Staper's mind at this time was to revive the old overland trade with India by way of Aleppo, which had made the fortunes of Venice in the Middle Ages. The difficulties

[1] Stevens invented a complicated system of transliteration, but it differs largely from the systems now in vogue, and is hard to follow. Canon V. G. Joshi has published some extracts (Bombay, 1912) in Marathi script with the old Konkani on one side, and a modern Marathi version opposite. The poetry of this remarkable work is really of a high order, e. g. the description of the Massacre of the Innocents (Joshi's ed., p. 7), and the author must have known Sanskrit to write as he did.

[2] I follow throughout J. Horton Ryley's *Ralph Fitch, England's Pioneer to India and Burma*, London, 1899, where all the documents bearing on the narrative are brought together.

in the way, were eventually found to be too great. The Portuguese at Ormuz, and the Spanish at Gibraltar, controlled the two strategic points on the route. Staper's mission to the East was, however, of singular importance, and rightly earned for him his epitaph in St. Helen's, Bishopsgate, where he is described as 'The greatest Merchant in his Tyme: the chiefest Actor in Discovere of the Trades of Turkey and East India'.[1] The moving spirit in the expedition to India was John Newbery, a traveller of great energy and experience. He was a good Arabic scholar, and had been to Tripolis twice before. In 1579 he had gone from that port to Syria, and in 1582 on a 'farre more long and dangerous voyage' through Turkey in Asia, as far as Ormuz, where he had made enemies. Immediately on his return he was requisitioned by Staper for his new venture. His companions were Ralph Fitch, also a merchant, William Leedes, a jeweller, and James Story, a painter. Newbery carried with him a letter of introduction to the Emperor Akbar from Queen Elizabeth which ran as follows:[2]

'Elizabeth by the grace of God etc. To the most invincible and most mightie prince, lord Zelabdim Echebar king of Cambaya. Invincible Emperor etc. The great affection which our subjects have to visit the most distant places of the world, not without good will and intention to introduce the trade of marchandize of al nations whatsoever they can, by which meanes the mutual and friendly trafique of marchandize on both sides may come, is the cause that the bearer of this letter John Newbery, jointly with those that be in his company, with a curteous and honest boldnesse, doe repaire to the borders and countreys of your Empire, we doubt not but that Your imperial Majestie through your royal grace will favorably and friendly accept him. And that you would doe it the rather for our sake to make us greatly beholding to your Majestie; wee should more earnestly, and with more wordes require it, if wee did think it needful. But by the singular report that is of your imperial Majesties humanitie in these uttermost parts of the world,[3] we are greatly eased

[1] Ryley, *op. cit.*, p. 230.

[2] Hakluyt, ed. MacLehose, v. 450, quoted by Ryley, p. 44.

[3] This is not an empty compliment. Mildenhall (Purchas, ii. 300) speaks of Akbar's kindness and tolerance to Christians as 'so much

of that burden, and therefore wee use the fewer and lesse words: onely we request that because they are our subjects, they may be honestly intreated and received. And that in respect of the hard journey which they have undertaken to places so far distant, it would please your Majestie with some libertie and securitie of voiage to gratifie it, with such privileges as to you shall seeme good: which curtesie if your Imperiall majestie shal to our subjects at our requests performe, wee, according to our royall honour, wil recompence the same with as many deserts as we can. And herewith we bid your Imperial Majestie to farewel.'

The party sailed for Tripolis on the ship *Tyger* on Shrove Tuesday 1583, an event echoed twenty years after in *Macbeth*.[1] On the *Tyger* were two other merchants bound for the East, William Shales and John Eldred. Eldred was a man of some note who afterwards made a fortune in trade with the East Indies, and it is he who furnished Hakluyt with the account of the early part of the journey upon which the present narrative is based.[2] The *Tyger* put into the harbour of Tripolis in Syria on May Day. The party then proceeded by caravan to Aleppo, which was reached on the 21st of the same month. Here they found a great number of traders of all nationalities, including Indians. Travelling on camel back to the Euphrates, they drifted down stream to Felugia,[3] suffering much from the rogueries of the river Arabs, who reminded the voyagers of the 'vagabond Egyptians' of their own country. It was now the middle of the hot season, and camels were hard to procure. Our travellers, however, packed their traps on donkey-back, and travelling by night to escape the blinding heat, eventually reached Bagdad. At Basra, four weeks' journey from Bagdad, Eldred and Shales stopped. Newbery and his party pushed on by ship to the great port of Ormuz, which they reached on September 5.

blazed throughout the world that it had come to the furthermost parts of the Ocean'.

[1] 'Her husband's to Aleppo gone, Master o' the *Tiger*' (*Macbeth*, II. iii). The reference may not, however, be specifically to any particular voyage. The *Tiger* (*Tyger*) was a well-known boat, which made many voyages to Tripoli and Alexandria. Her owner was Alderman Martins and her master, Thomas Rickman.

[2] Ryley, pp. 217–18.

[3] Feluja, on the Euphrates north-west of Bagdad.

Ormuz, then the key of the Persian Gulf, had been taken and fortified by Albuquerque in 1515, and the ruins of its fortress, bombarded and stormed by the English in 1622, may still be seen, though its trade has long since passed to Bandar Abbas. Here they hoped to found a factory,[1] and started a shop, ostensibly for trade in cloth, saffron, glass, knives, and small-ware. In reality they invested considerable sums in jewels,[2] particularly the famous Bahrein pearls which could be procured locally at a cheap rate under the expert guidance of Leedes, though they were obliged to do this secretly for fear of being robbed.

Here, however, disaster overtook them. Traders of foreign nationality looked upon these newcomers with jealousy and suspicion, and among them was a Venetian named Michael Stropene, whose enmity Newbery had somehow incurred on his former visit to Ormuz. Stropene had been warned by his brother at Aleppo of the Englishmen's coming.[3] He denounced them to the Captain of the Castle, Don Mathias de Albuquerque,[4] as spies, carrying letters from the Pretender Don Antonio. The Portuguese had an additional cause to hate the presence of the English in the East, as reports had just arrived that Drake had fired on a Portuguese vessel in the Spice Islands, and gone off with a cargo of cloves.[5] The Governor, however, was an honest man and a friend of Newbery's. He refused to punish them, but as the charges demanded investigation, he decided to refer the matter to the Viceroy at Goa.

He determined, therefore, to put the party under arrest, and to dispatch them by the next boat to Goa; meanwhile, they were allowed to trade under surveillance, and did very well. Newbery contrived to send a letter back to Eldred at Basra,[6] imploring him to move the English Government to take the matter up, for he did not know what might be their

[1] Linschoten's story in Ryley, pp. 68–70.

[2] Newbery's share in the adventure was £400 (Eldred in Ryley, p. 218).

[3] Newbery's letter in Ryley, p. 76.

[4] So Fitch in Ryley, p. 56. Linschoten, *ibid.*, p. 69, calls the Captain of Ormuz Don Gonzalo de Menzes. Apparent discrepancies of this kind constantly occur in the different narratives. Fitch is, of course, the best authority on his own adventures. Don Mathias de Albuquerque was afterwards (1591–7) Viceroy of Goa (Fonseca, p. 90).

[5] *Ibid.*, p. 78.

[6] Given by Ryley, p. 75.

fate at Goa. 'It may be they will cut our throats, or keep us long in prison.' The party sailed on October 11, touching at Diu, Daman, Bassein, Thana, and Chaul en route, Goa being reached on November 29.[1] Fitch notes with surprise the usual marvels of Indian life, which fill the pages of contemporary travel *ad nauseam*—animal hospitals, *sati*, the sacred cow, the *tadi* palm, and the Brahmins.[2]

At Goa, however, our travellers did not meet with the savage treatment they feared. They had probably, like many other Englishmen of Elizabeth's time, been brought up in the Old Faith, and they wisely 'behaved themselves very Catholikely and devoute, everie day hearing Mass with Beades in their hands'. The Jesuits regarded them, indeed, with suspicion, and advised that they should either be compelled to join the Order or be shipped off to Lisbon for trial. It is hinted that the Jesuits also had designs upon their money, which would, if the Englishmen entered their Order, become the property of the Society: however this may be, only one of them yielded. This was James Story, the painter, who was admitted as a novice to the monastery of St. Paul, and was employed in decorating the magnificent churches with which the city abounded.

Meanwhile, the prisoners found some good friends, and were well treated. 'Had it not pleased God', writes Newbery,[3] 'to put into the minds of the archbishop and two other Padres or Jesuits of St. Paul's colledge[4] to stand our friends, we might have rotted in prison. The archbishop is a very good man, who hath two young men to his servantes, the one of them was borne at Hamborough and is called Bernard Borgers: and the other was borne at Enchuysen, whose name is John Linscot,[5] who did us great pleasure: for by them the

[1] Ryley, p. 65. On p. 62 it is the 20th (probably a misprint).

[2] '*A kind of craftie people, worse than the Jews*,' Fitch observes in another place! But perhaps he means here the Banyans.

[3] His last letter, to Leonard Poore, Ryley, pp. 78–9.

[4] Described by Fonseca, p. 260.

[5] John Huyghen van Linschoten, born at Haarlem 1563 (*not* Enkhuizen as the text has it), came out to Goa with the archbishop and stayed there 1583–9. He published his *Itineratio*, one of the best books on India written up to that time, 1595–6. This work was translated into many

archbishop was many times put in minde of us. And the two good fathers of S. Paul who travelled very much for us, the one of them is called Padre Marke, who was borne in Bruges in Flanders, and the other was borne in Wiltshire in England and is called Padre Thomas Stevens.' Thus on December 22 they were set at liberty, 'putting in sureties for two thousand ducats[1] not to depart the town'. The surety's name was Andreas Taborer and he was found by Father Stevens.

But the party did not think it safe to stay longer in Goa than they could help.

'We made sute to the Viceroy and Justice', says Fitch, 'to have our money againe, considering that they had had it in their hands neere five moneths and could proove nothing against us. The Viceroy made us a very sharpe answere, and sayde wee should be better sifted before it were long, and that they had further matter against us. Whereupon we presently determined rather to seeke our liberties, than to bee in danger for ever to be slaves in the country, for it was told us we should have Ye strapado.'[2]

Newbery, Fitch, and Leedes, therefore, on April 5, 1585, arranged a picnic in the country, leaving a Dutch boy in charge of their shop.[3] Thence, by the help of a *patimar*[4] they escaped to Belgaum. The Jesuits were very angry, and Padre Marke called them 'heretics, spies, and a thousand other railing speeches'.[5] Storey had not joined in the escape, but he refused to stay any longer in the monastery. He married a 'Mestico's[6] daughter of the town' and settled down there. Fitch, Newbery, and Leedes travelled through Bijapur, Golconda (where they did some business in stones), and so on to Ujjain. Finally they journeyed to Agra, 'a very great city and populous, built with stone, having fair and

languages, among them being English in 1598. It has been edited by Burnell and Tiele for the Hakluyt Society. Linschoten died in 1610.

[1] The Venetseander or Venetian ducat, equivalent to 6*s*. 8*d*. sterling. Linschoten says 2,000 *pardaos*, or half this sum.

[2] Fitch *apud* Ryley, p. 62.

[3] Linschoten *apud* Ryley, p. 73.

[4] 'One of the Indian postes which in winter times caryeth letters', *ibid*.

[5] He said 'hee once had in his hands . . . of theirs a bagge wherein was 40,000 Venetseanders'. This was a gross exaggeration.

[6] i.e. a half-caste.

large streets, with a fair river running by it, which falleth into the gulf of Bengala. It hath a fair castle and a strong, with a very fair ditch'. From Agra they went to Fathpur Sikri, and were struck with the prosperity of the country and the splendour of the Court. All the way from Agra to Fathpur was 'a market of victuals and other things, as full as though a man were still in a town, and so many people as if a man were in a market'. Both cities were 'much greater than London and very populous'. In the royal stables were '1,000 elephants, 30,000 horses, 1,400 tame deer, and such store of ounces, tigers, buffles, cocks and hawks that is very strange to see'. In the royal harem were eight hundred concubines. In the markets was 'a great resort of merchants from Persia and out of India, and very much merchandize of silk and cloth and of precious stones, both rubies, diamonds, and pearls'. No wonder the travellers were impressed with the commercial possibilities of India. Apparently they interviewed Akbar, for Fitch describes the great monarch as simply attired in 'a white *cabie* (or tunic), made like a shirt tied with strings on one side, and a little cloth on his head, coloured oftentimes with red or yellow'. But of the details of the interview or the delivery of Elizabeth's letter, Fitch tells us nothing. At Fathpur they stayed till September 28, 1585. William Leedes entered Akbar's service, 'who did entertain him very well and gave him an house and five slaves, an horse, and every day six shillings in money'. 'Then Master John Newbery took his journey toward the city of Lahore, determining from thence to go for Persia, and then for Aleppo or Constantinople, whether he could get soonest passage unto, and directed me to go for Bengala and for Pegu, and did promise me, if it pleased God, to meet me in Bengala within two years with a ship out of England.' This is the last we hear of that intrepid pioneer. 'He dyed in his travels', Purchas notes, 'unknown how and where', the first of the many Englishmen who have perished in the quest of new scenes of adventure and conquest in the East. Fitch was now alone. He travelled to the mouth of the Ganges, and visited Bassein, Pegu, and Malacca, making inquiries about trade and about the route to China and Japan. Returning to Bengal and hearing nothing of Newbery, he resolved to go home. He started in 1589, and travelled via Ceylon, Goa (where he was, curiously enough, not arrested), Ormuz, and Aleppo, reaching England on April 29, 1591. So ended the first organized English expedition to India. The knowledge obtained was of great value, and largely brought about the foundation of the East India Company.

A NOTE ON AUTHORITIES

(1) *Father Stevens.* The only complete account is in the introduction to Saldanha's edition of the *Christian Purana.* Other notices are in the *Dictionary of National Biography*, Supplement iii, p. 355, by A. F. Pollard; a note in Gray and Bell's edition of Pyrard de Laval's *Travels* (Hakluyt Society), ii. 269; a note by F. M. Mascareñhas in *Indian Antiquary*, 1878, p. 117; and Monier Williams, 'Facts of Indian Progress,' *Contemporary Review*, April 1878.[1] He is often confused with his brother Richard; e. g. he cannot, as is usually stated, have taken his degree at Oxford in 1577, if he went to Rome in 1575, and thence to Goa.

(2) *Newbery.* Hakluyt gives five letters from Newbery; namely (1) from Aleppo to himself, May 28, 1583, (2) from Aleppo to Leonard Poore, May 29, 1583, (3) from Babylon (Bagdad) to the same, July 20, 1583, (4) 'From out the prison at Ormuz' to Eldred and Shales, September 21–24, 1583, asking for help, (5) from Goa to Leonard Poore, January 20, 1584. To these must be added Eldred's letters (1) from Bagdad, July 14, 1583, (2) from Basra, November 6, 1583, forwarding Newbery's appeal for help, (3) from Basra, January 22, 1584, announcing that Newbery and his friends were prisoners at Goa. The above correspondence was all found among the papers of William Hareborne, our ambassador at Constantinople.

(3) *Fitch.* Hakluyt gives Fitch's narration of his adventures, and a letter to Poore, sent along with Newbery's last letter.

(4) *Linschoten.* Linschoten's *Itineratio* (English translation edited by Burnell and Tiele for the Hakluyt Society) gives a long account of the party's adventures in Goa. It differs in many minor points of detail from Fitch. The whole of the information is collected in Ryley's work referred to above, where it can be most conveniently consulted.

[1] A complete list is given in the *D. N. B.* article referred to.

CHAPTER III

THE FOUNDATION OF THE COMPANY AND HAWKINS'S MISSION TO SURAT

In 1588, the defeat of the Armada finally destroyed the legend of the invincibility of the Catholic powers by sea. England was now the open enemy of the Papacy, and the Vatican decree, instead of restraining her sailors, was an incentive to them to push on to the Indies. The spell that lay upon the Eastern seas had already been broken by Drake and Cavendish. The old Levant Company suffered severely from the Spanish cruisers which harassed their fleets from the harbour of Gibraltar. English merchants had felt keenly the Spanish invasion of the Netherlands, which ruined the great mart of Antwerp,[1] and even when the Dutch recovered their prestige, they proved not friends but dangerous rivals. Their action in 1597, when they suddenly raised the price of pepper from 3*s*. to 8*s*. per pound, caused much feeling in England.[2] All these circumstances combined to create a strong desire to find a sea-route to India, which would make England independent of her neighbours, and enable her to fetch merchandise from the East for herself. At the same time, men's appetites were whetted by reports of the 'wealth of Ormuz and of Ind'. Father Stevens's letter and Fitch's wonderful narrative had been eagerly read. Linschoten's great work was translated into English, and reports from Dr. Thorne of Seville were circulated.[3] In 1592 Sir John Borrough captured the *Madre de Dios*, with its valuable *Matricola*, or catalogue of the Portuguese colonies.[4] Expeditions to the

[1] The Merchants of the Staple and the Merchant Adventurers had 'houses' in Bruges and Antwerp, and no doubt these suffered severely. See e.g. *The Beginnings of English Overseas Enterprise*, by Sir C. P. Lucas, Oxford, 1917, *passim*.

[2] See Birdwood, *Report on Old Records*, p. 179; Macpherson, *History of European Commerce*, p. 77.

[3] Markham, *Lancaster Voyages* (Hakluyt Society), 1877, p. 2.

[4] Similar though less detailed documents were taken on the *Saint Philip* by Drake in 1587.

Indies by the Cape route were now all the rage. As early as 1590, John Davis set out in the *Samaritan*, but got no farther than Madeira. In the next year, John Raymond sailed from Plymouth Sound with three tall ships, the *Penelope*, the *Merchant Royal*, and the *Edward Bonaventure*, bound for 'divers Islands and Regions in the East Indies'. It was July before they made the Cape of Good Hope, when the *Merchant Royal* was sent back with fifty men, unfit, owing to scurvy, to go farther. Then, off Cape Corrientes, the *Penelope* was lost with all hands. Captain Lancaster with the *Bonaventure* was now left alone, and underwent a series of strange adventures. After plundering merchant vessels in the Arabian Sea and off Galle, he turned home, but being without maps or proper instruments, drifted right across the Atlantic to Trinidad. Here the *Bonaventure* anchored; one night, while the bulk of the crew were ashore, she broke adrift from her moorings with only five men and a boy aboard, but managed to reach England. Of the rest of the crew, some were killed by the Spaniards; others broke their necks trying to catch sea-fowl, and the rest, including the captain, were saved by some French vessels, and reached home in May 1594. Only 25 out of the 97 who originally sailed from Plymouth saw their native shores again, but the booty and spices in the hold of the *Bonaventure* showed men what riches lay in store.[1] In 1596, another fleet, consisting of the *Bear*, the *Bear's Whelp*, and the *Benjamin*, was sent out by Sir Robert Dudley, with an introductory letter from Queen Elizabeth to the Emperor of China. They were never seen again. According to an obscure report, they waylaid and plundered some Portuguese galleons, but were in their turn exterminated by their rivals.[2]

England was now contemplating peace with Spain. Essex's raid in 1596 had convinced us of the futility of carrying on a war against a great continental power without an army,

[1] See for the story, *The Lancaster Voyages*.

[2] Purchas, *Pilgrimes*, ii. 289 ff., where an intercepted report from the Judge of Commission at Puerto Rico is quoted. Four survivors were shipwrecked on an adjacent island. Three were killed by the Spaniards for loot, and the fourth was taken prisoner and poisoned. See also Macpherson, *op. cit.*, pp. 76–7.

and the death of Philip II, two years later, removed our most inveterate foe. Accordingly the great London merchants, the Lord Mayor, Sir Edward Osborne, Thomas Smythe, and Sir Richard Staper, with other members of the old Levant Company, jealous at the success of the Dutch, wished to come to some understanding about the exclusive claims of Spain and Portugal to trade with the New World. Refusing to recognize the Bull of 1493 and its corollaries, they demanded the privilege of trading with any Eastern nation where they had not already been forestalled by their rivals. They accordingly drew up and presented to the Privy Council through Sir Francis Walsingham a long document entitled *Certain reasons why the English merchants may trade into the East Indies, especially to such rich kingdoms and dominions as are not subject to the King of Spain and Portugal: together with the true limits of the Portugal conquest and jurisdiction in these oriental parts.*[1] The Privy Council referred the matter to Foulke Greville, the learned friend of Sir Philip Sidney. Greville drafted a long answer, ' made out of Osorius,[2] Eden's Decads,[3] and specially out of the voyages of John Huyghen ', which is a most curious and interesting epitome of what was then known about the voyage to the East round the Cape. This document is dated March 10, 1599, but it was not until December 31, 1600, that the charter, entitled *A privilege for fifteen years granted by Her Majesty to certain adventurers for the discovery of the trade for the East Indies*, was finally issued.[4]

Sir Thomas Smythe, having secured this charter, sent round the beadle with the Company's subscription-book for the first voyage. After some trouble, capital to the amount of £68,323 was raised, and a fleet of four ships, the *Red Dragon*, *Hector*, *Ascension*, and *Susan*, was fitted out, altogether 1,400 tons, with a complement of 480 men. Captain James Lancaster

[1] Bruce, *Annals of the East India Company*, i. 116 ff.

[2] Jeronymo Osorio de Fonseca, Bishop of Silves, 1561. Transl. Gibbs, London, 1752.

[3] Referred to in the letter as ' John Barros, his three decads of Asia '. Barros was Historiographer Royal at Lisbon. His chronicle goes down to 1526: De Couto carries it on to 1580.

[4] The original is lost. For copies, see *First Letter Book of the East India Company*, p. 163; Purchas, *Pilgrimes*, ii. 361.

was in charge. With the adventures of this fleet at Achin in Sumatra and at Bantam (where they established a factory), we are not here concerned. The second voyage was a repetition of the first. Meanwhile, however, the idea of getting into touch with the mainland of India, as suggested by Fitch, had not been forgotten. It was determined to send another embassy to the court of Akbar, to be followed later, if necessary, by a fleet.[1]

John Mildenhall, who was chosen for this errand, travelled to India by the overland route through northern Persia. He took his own time over the journey, and did not reach Lahore until 1603. On reaching Agra, he was kindly received at first by Akbar, until the Jesuit mission, perceiving the dangers of Protestant rivalry to the ascendancy which they had gained over the Emperor, commenced the bitter opposition to an English alliance which they maintained so unswervingly throughout the next reign. On being asked by Akbar what they knew about the English, 'they flatly answered', says Mildenhall, 'that our Nation were all thieves, and that I was a spy sent thither for no other purpose to have friendship with His Majesty, but that afterwards our men might come thither and get some of his ports, and so put His Majesty to much trouble.'[2] They further hindered negotiations by bribing his interpreter to abscond; but Mildenhall learnt Persian, and according to his own story, scored a brilliant diplomatic victory, 'to my own great contentment, and as I hope, to the profit of my nation'. Accordingly, Akbar ordered that 'whatever privileges or commandments he would have, should be presently written, sealed and given, without any more delay or question'. Unfortunately, the *farman* was not forthcoming, and it is difficult to avoid the conclusion that Mildenhall was a rascal who did not scruple to invent whatever he thought might please his employers. Staper apparently thought the same, for a note in the Company's minutes for 1609 states that his application for further employment was

[1] The bulk of what follows is taken from the author's paper on William Hawkins in the *Bhandarkar Commemoration Volume*.

[2] See his letter to Staper 'from Casbin in Persia, Oct. 3, 1606' in Purchas, ii. 299.

rejected as he was ' not thought fit to be engaged '. He came to a bad end, for we learn from the diary of one Nicholas Withington, preserved by Purchas, that he ' had been employed with three English young men, which he poisoned in Persia to make himself master of their goods, but he was likewise poisoned, yet by preservations lived for many months after, but swelled exceedingly, and so came to Agra with the value of 20,000 dollars '.[1] Here he died early in 1614, having, as the Jesuits told Withington, ' given all his goods to a French Protestant to marry his bastard daughter in Persia and bring up another '.[2] The Company employed Withington, Steele, and others to recover property belonging to them, with partial success.

The East India Company did not, however, abandon the project. The first two ' voyages ' had, as we have seen, gone to the Spice Islands. When the third fleet made ready to sail, it was determined that one vessel should be sent to Surat, to establish a factory there by treaty with the Mughal Court, buy calicoes, and rejoin the rest at Bantam ; by which means, writes Captain Keeling, the ' General ' of the expedition, they ' would lay the best foundation for gain against another year that ever I heard of '.[3] Surat was chosen for many reasons. As the great entrepôt of the Mughal Empire on the western coast of India, it was, in the words of a contemporary traveller, ' a city of very great trade in all classes of merchandize, a very important sea-port, yielding a large revenue to the king and frequented by many ships from Malabar and all parts '. The Portuguese had recognized this, and in 1530–1, Antonio de Silveira burnt the ships in the harbour and raided the town. Since its conquest by Akbar in 1573, however, they had left it alone, and hence it did not come under the Company's agreement not to trade with any place 'in lawful and actual possession of any Christian prince at amity with England, who would not accept of such trade '.

[1] Purchas, iv. 173. Withington came out with Captain Best in the Tenth Voyage.

[2] His tomb exists in the old Roman Catholic cemetery at Agra (*J.R.A.S.*, 1910, p. 495).

[3] Purchas, vi. 59.

The ambassador selected for this mission was William Hawkins, a nephew of the great Sir John, the terror of the Spanish Main. He was one of eleven children, two of whom, besides himself, were connected with the East India Company.[1] He had seen fighting under Fenton off Brazil and had been in the Levant, where he learnt Turkish.[2] Hawkins sailed as master of the *Hector* from Erith on March 8, 1607. Captain Keeling, on the *Dragon*, accompanied him as 'General'. A third ship, the *Consent*, Captain David Middleton, sailed independently,[3] and it was well for them that they did, for they reached the Cape on July 27, whereas Keeling did not make it until December 17.[4] He had been blown right out of his course to the Brazil coast, and owing to scurvy and lack of water was forced to put into Sierra Leone to refit. Here an interesting event is recorded by Keeling. On September 5 the crew of the *Hector* acted the tragedy of *Hamlet*. On the 30th Captain Keeling asked Hawkins to dinner, 'where my companions acted *King Richard II*'; and on the following day he again 'envited Captain Hawkins to a ffishe dinner, and had *Hamlet* acted abord me, wch I p'mitt to keepe my people from idleness and unlawful games, or sleepe'.[5] The voyage was altogether very long and tedious. Socotra was only reached in March 1608. Here, acting on the advice of some friendly Gujarati sailors, they awaited the bursting of the south-west monsoon. On June 24 they parted, Keeling for Bantam and Hawkins for Surat, armed with a duplicate of the Commission under the Great Seal. He arrived on August 4, and came ashore on the 28th. The following interesting description of Surat as they found

[1] Giles Hawkins was a factor at Bantam; Charles was a partner in the Sixth Voyage (Markham, *The Hawkins Voyages*, p. xlii *n*.).

[2] *Ibid*., p. xliv.

[3] She left Tilbury on March 12 (Purchas, iii. 51; cf. his marginal note, ii. 502).

[4] Keeling's Diary in Purchas, ii. 508.

[5] So Rundall, in *Narratives of Voyages to the North-West* (Hakluyt Society), p. 231. This was published in 1849. Since then some one has stolen the page from Keeling's manuscript diary. For plays on board ship, cf. *The Lancaster Voyages*, p. 147, where Sir Henry Middleton at Cape Verde 'had a great feast and a play played', on the *Trades Increase*, June 18, 1610.

SURAT FORT FROM RIVERSIDE

it, from the pen of William Finch, one of the company, is preserved by Purchas:[1]

'The city is of good quantity, with many fair Merchants' houses therein, standing twenty miles within the land upon a fair river. Some three miles from the south of the river, (where on the south side lieth a small low island overflowed in time of rain), is the bar, where ships trade and unlade, whereon at springtide is three fathom water. Over this the channel is fair to the city side, able to bear vessels of fifty tons laden. The river runs to Bramport (*Burhanpur*), others say to Musselpatan. As you come up to the river, on the right hand stands the Castle, well walled and ditched, reasonable great and fair, with a number of fair pieces, some of them of exceeding greatness. It hath one gate to the Greenward, with a drawbridge and a small port on the river-side. The captain hath in command two hundred horse. Before this lieth the Medon (*Maidan*), which is a pleasant green, in the midst whereof is a May pole to hang lights on and for other pastimes on great Festivals.[2]

'On this side the city lieth open to the Green, but on all other parts is ditched and fenced with thick hedges, having three gates, of which one leadeth to Variaw,[3] a small village where is the ford to pass over to Cambaya way. Near this village on the left hand lieth a small Aldea (village) on the river-bank, very pleasant, where stands a great Pagoda, much resorted to by the Indians. Another gate leadeth to Bramport, a third to Nonsary (*Navsari*) a town ten cose (*kos*, two miles) off, where is made a great store of calico, having a fair river [4] coming to it. Some ten cose further lieth Gondoree [5] and a little further, Belsaca,[6] the frontier town upon Daman.

'Hard without Nonsary gate is a fair tank,[7] sixteen square, enclosed on all sides with stone steps, three-quarters of an English mile in compass, with a small house in the middest. On the further side are diverse fair tombs with a goodly paved court, pleasant to behold; behind which groweth a small grove of mango-trees, whither the citizens go forth to banquet. Some half cose behind this place is a great tree much worshipped by the Banians, where they affirm a Dew (*Deva*, god) to keep, and that it hath often times been cut

[1] iv. 27 ff.
[2] Probably a *dīpmāl* or lampstand.
[3] A hamlet on the north side of the town.
[4] The Purna River.
[5] Probably Gandevi.
[6] Bulsār.
[7] The Gopi Talão (now drained).

down and stocked up at the Moores' command and yet hath sprung up again. Near to the Castle is the Alphandica (*alphandega*, customs house), where is a pair of stairs for lading and unlading of goods: within are rooms for keeping goods till they are cleared, the custom being two and half for goods, three for victuals, and two for money. Without the gate is a great Gondoree or Bazaar. Right before this gate stands a tree within an arbour, whereon the Fokeers (*fakirs*), which are Indian holy men, sit in state. Betwixt this and the Castle, on the entrance of the Green, is the market for horse and cattle. A little lower, on the right over the river, is a little pleasant town, Ranele,[1] inhabited by a people called Naites,[2] speaking another language, and for the most part seamen: the houses are fair therein, with fair steps to each man's door, the streets narrow. They are very friendly to the English. Here are many pleasant Gardens, which attract many to pass there their time: and on the trees are an infinite number of great Bats which we saw at Saint Augustine's, hanging by the claws on the boughs, making a shrill noise. This fowl, the people say, engendereth in the ear: on each wing it hath an hook, and giveth the young suck.'

Hawkins landed and was politely received by the local authorities, who, however, referred his case to 'Mocreb chan', or Mukarrab Khan, the Governor of Cambay and Surat, afterwards known to the English as their most relentless opponent. The messenger to Cambay was delayed by the violence of the monsoon; meanwhile, in spite of some opposition, Hawkins started to trade in such articles as might be profitably sold at Bantam; for it was decided to send the *Hector* to join Keeling as agreed on, while Hawkins himself went to Agra to present his petition. The *Hector* was soon loaded up. Master Marlowe was put in command and farewells were said and Hawkins returned to his work at Surat, when 'the next day,[3] going about my affairs to the great man's brother, I met with some ten or twelve of our men, of the better sort of them, very much frighted, telling me the heaviest news, as I thought, that ever came unto me, of the

[1] Rander (called Ranel by Barbosa).

[2] *Nayata*, Arab merchants and sailors who settled there in 1225. Cf. Stanley's Barbosa, p. 67.

[3] October 2. The passage is from Hawkins's diary, *apud* Purchas, iii. 4.

taking of the barks by a Portugal frigate[1] or two, and all goods and men taken, only they escaped'. Finch[2] gives further details.

'These frigates were Portugals, which desired one come to talk with them, and Master Bucke rashly doing it, they detained him, and after (I and Nicholas Ufflet being ashore) Master Marlowe and the rest began to flee; the cockswain would have fought, which he would not permit, but running aground through ignorance of the channel, they were taken going on the sandy island by Portugal treachery, and the fault of some of themselves,[3] nineteen with Master Bucke; but the Ginne put off the Pinnace, and notwithstanding the Portugal bullets, rowed her to Surat. Four escaped by swimming and got that night to Surat, besides Nicholas Ufflet and myself, near twenty miles from the place.'

It subsequently transpired that the *Hector* herself had got away, only the longboat and her crew being captured; but Hawkins found himself in an awkward plight. He was surrounded by enemies. Mukarrab Khan, instigated by the Portuguese, tried to kidnap him and steal his goods. He decided that his best course was to lay his case before the Emperor at Agra; and on February 1, 1609, he set out for the capital, leaving Finch, who was down with dysentery, to look after his goods at Surat.

After sundry attempts had been made to murder him *en route*, Hawkins presented himself to Jahangir on April 16 at Agra. The king was pleased to see him, and Hawkins found that he could make himself understood in Turkish, which is not far removed from Turki, the ancestral tongue of the descendants of Babur. Jahangir liked new acquaintances, especially good fellows who could hold their liquor, and Hawkins entertained him vastly with stories of his travels. No wonder the 'Portugalls', who since the time of

[1] See p. 52, note 2.
[2] Finch, *apud* Purchas, iv. 20.
[3] So Hawkins. But the Company thought otherwise. 'We are informed by Bucke and Marlowe', they write, 'that they were destitute of powder and other means to defend themselves, which was a great neglect in your part to be so secure as not to arm and animate your men thoroughly' (*First Letter Book*, p. 316). These men were taken from Goa to the Trunk at Lisbon where they remained till 1610, in great want (*ibid.*, p. 306). Their crime was 'trading in the East without the king of Spain's licence'.

Akbar had held a distinguished position at the court, became like 'madde dogges'. Hawkins, Nicholas Ufflet, and the 'boy', Stephen Gravener, became mysteriously ill, and the latter died. Thereupon Jahangir gave his friend a wife out of the royal harem to cook his food, and so avoid untoward accidents in the future. This lady was a daughter of Mubarik Shah, an Armenian Christian who had risen to distinction in Akbar's service. The marriage service was read by Ufflet, until such time as a more formal ceremony could be performed by a regular chaplain. The king now seemed quite won over. He gave Hawkins his commission, written under his Golden Seal, to be sent to Surat, together with a stinging reproof to Mukarrab Khan for his bad behaviour to the English. Hawkins was now in high glee; he was with the king day and night (usually until the World Grasper was removed, the worse for drink, to the harem); at the audience, he stood within the coveted Red Rails; and Jahangir, in an outburst of friendship, went so far as to offer him, if he would stay at the court, a pension of £3,200 a year, a troop of horse, and any concessions for the factory that he liked to ask! Finding, like Philip II of Spain, that 'Achins' was a difficult name to pronounce, Jahangir gave him the title of 'Inglis Khan' ('in Persia, it is the title for a Duke', Hawkins parenthetically explains). In all of which, our envoy, seeing that 'it would feather my nest and do Your Worships a service', as he writes to his masters, cheerfully acquiesced.

His triumph, however, was destined to be short-lived. The nobles and the 'Portugalls' were consumed with jealousy. The Viceroy of Goa sent a letter (accompanied by a handsome present) warning Jahangir that if the English got a footing in the country, he would eventually lose his harbours and his trade altogether.[1] This, according to Hawkins, was the cause of his downfall. 'The king went from his word, esteeming a few toys which the Fathers had promised him

[1] The Viceroy was De Mendosa. He treated Jahangir's concession as an act of war. Father Pinheiro, one of the Jesuit missionaries at Agra, acted as intermediary between Jahangir and De Mendosa's successor Tavora, and got the concessions reversed (V. A. Smith, *Oxford History of India*, 1919, pp. 379–80).

more than his honour.' 'It is true', His Majesty cynically remarked, 'that the commandment for the Factory was sealed and ready to be delivered; but upon letters received from Mocrebcan, and better consideration had on the affairs of his ports in Guzerat, he thought it fitting not to let him have it.' Unfortunately for Hawkins there was another Englishman at Agra who kept a journal, and he supplements the story in a very different fashion, though, as there was no love lost between the two, we must, perhaps, allow something for the writer's malice. This was John Jourdain [1] of the *Ascension*, which, with the *Union*,[2] had set out in 1608 on the Company's Fourth Voyage, and had been wrecked on the shoals in the Gulf of Cambay. The survivors had found their way to Surat, where, owing to the lack of control exercised by the Master, Captain Sharpeigh, they had been involved in various broils,[3] and had finally set out for Agra. Jourdain says that Hawkins had at first acquired popularity at Court by winning the favour of Asaf Khan, a powerful nobleman, whose sister was the famous Nur Jahan, afterwards Jahangir's wife. After a while, however, by trying to drive a hard bargain in trade, Hawkins offended the Queen Mother and Khwaja Abul Hassan, the Chief Secretary. Abul Hassan took his revenge in an amusing fashion. The king was a great drinker, but was ashamed of his vice, and cruelly punished those who talked of his orgies or of the part they took in them.

'The king', says Jourdain, 'was informed that some of his great men were bibbers of wine and that before they came to the Court daily, they filled their heads with strong drink, and commanded that upon pain of his displeasure none of his nobles that came to his court should drink any strong drink before their coming. Now Abdelhasan, knowing that Hawkins was a great drinker, feed the porter (as is supposed) to smell if he had drunk any strong drink, which is easily

[1] For details, see his Journal, edited by Foster for the Hakluyt Society, Series II, vol. xvi.

[2] The *Union* went on to Achin. After a disastrous voyage she went on the rocks off Audierne in Brittany on her return journey.

[3] One Tom Tucker had got drunk and killed a calf. This enraged the 'Banyans', who paid a handsome sum to the authorities every year to stop cow-killing. Captain Downton found it impossible to open a beef market for the same reason (Downton in Purchas, iv. 220).

discerned by one that is fasting. So the chief porter finding that Hawkins had drunk, he presently carried him before the king in presence of the whole Court, where, by the mouth of Abdelhasan, being Secretary, it was told the king he had drunk strong drink. Whereat the king paused a little space, and considering that he was a stranger, he bid him go to his house, and when he came next he should not drink. So being disgraced in public, he could not be suffered to come into his accustomed place near the king, which was the cause why he went not so often to Court.'[1]

Whether this was true or not, Hawkins was now out of favour. 'Stay I would not, among these worthless infidels,' he writes, but unfortunately Mrs. Hawkins's relatives objected to her leaving India. At first he thought of asking the Jesuits (who were ready to do anything to get rid of him) to give him a passport to settle in Goa, with full liberty of conscience, and eventually returning to England when opportunity offered. Jourdain, however, pointed out the dangers of this. News had come of the appearance of a fresh English fleet off the coast of Cambay, and Jourdain proposed to go and join it.

'I told him', he writes, 'if he went to Goa his life would not be long, because he had much disputed against the Pope and their religion, and was apt to do the like again there, if he were urged thereunto, which would cost him his life, and the sooner because of his goods. But he answered that the Fathers had promised to get him a pass from the Viceroy, and also from the Bishop and priests, that he might use his own conscience. I told him the same cause would be his destruction, if he went. So he was persuaded to go that way and I was persuaded to go the other way, although he urged me very far, promising great wages; but his promises were of little force, for he was very fickle in his resolution, as also in his religion, for in his house he used altogether the custom of the Moors or Mahometans and seemed to be discontent if all men did not the like.'

With this malicious hit, Jourdain parted from Hawkins on July 28, 1611, and reached Surat in October.

[1] Jourdain's Journal, p. 104 ff. Hawkins was lucky. Some unfortunate nobles, after a banquet to welcome the Persian ambassadors, boasted of the 'merry night past'. For this Jahangir had them flogged almost to death (*Embassy of Sir Thos. Roe*, ed. Foster, pp. 303–4).

We must now turn back for a short time. In 1609 the Company, after a period of deep depression at the loss of the *Ascension* and the *Union*, had recovered its spirits owing to the success of Captain Middleton's voyage in the *Consent*. In 1609 they equipped the sixth voyage on a scale which they had not yet attempted. £82,000 was subscribed, and they built at Deptford a splendid new vessel, the *Trades Increase*, of 1,100 tons. The king himself launched it, and gave Sir Thomas Smythe a medal in honour of the occasion.[1] It was now fitted out in charge of Sir Henry Middleton, the other vessels being the *Peppercorne*, Captain Downton, and the *Darling*.[2] Besides Middleton, the *Trades Increase* carried one Lawrence Femmell as chief factor; he was probably sent to protect the Company's interests, and was cordially disliked. Middleton and Femmel had detailed orders as to their procedure, for nothing was spared to make the voyage a success. Journals were to be kept, giving details about trade, coinage, weights and measures, and the character of the inhabitants of the various ports. 'Civil behaviour' to natives on the part of the crew was enjoined.

Blasphemy, swearing, drunkenness, and gambling were to be punished, as 'calculated to provoke divine vengeance'. For similar reasons, the captains were to be 'very careful to assemble together their whole family every morning and evening, and to join together in all humility with hearty prayer to Almighty God for His merciful protection and favour'. They were to go to Socotra, Aden, and Mocha, thence to Surat, where they were to get into touch with Hawkins and ascertain what privileges he had obtained. At Surat they were to do their best to establish a factory, and obtain the privilege of trading free of duty. In all things they were to uphold 'the honour of our King and the reputation of our traffick'. Strict economy was to be observed in firing salutes: wages were not to be raised: there was to be no private trade and no carrying of passengers. Their cargo

[1] *Calendar of State Papers*, 1513–1616, para. 476.

[2] The details of the voyage are given from the original manuscripts in the India Office in the *Lancaster Voyages* (ed. Markham for the Hakluyt Society) which I follow throughout. The spelling is modernized.

consisted of cloth, lead, red lead, tin, quicksilver, vermilion, sword-blades, kerseys, and red caps. They were to load up with indigo, calico, cotton yarn, cinnamon, sandal, ginger, opium, gum benjamin, olibanum, aloes, and lac. They were to sell their iron, lead, calico, and cloth at Priaman and Bantam, where silk, gold, and above all pepper (400 tons if they could), were to be loaded; but too much anxiety for pepper was not to be displayed, for fear of putting up the price. Rare birds and beasts, for the Company's patrons, were to be bought.

They started on April 1, 1610. The Cape was reached at the end of July. At St. Augustine's Bay they met the ill-fated *Union* of the Fourth Voyage, and gave her much-needed victuals. Socotra was made in October and Aden on November 7. Here the conduct of the Arabs was suspicious, but Middleton pressed on to Mocha, leaving behind Captain Downton with the *Peppercorne*. The Turkish Governor of Aden refused to trade and imprisoned two parties which went ashore, whereupon Downton went to Mocha to join his chief. Here he found that Middleton had been treacherously seized with fifty-eight of his crew, and it was not until May that, making their guards drunk, they escaped. Middleton was furious, but could do nothing, so he went on to Surat, where equally evil luck awaited him. The coast was blockaded by Don Francisco da Soto, the Portuguese Captain Major, with eighteen frigates, and he refused to allow the English to approach. Letters from Hawkins were, however, smuggled aboard. Presently Jourdain appeared, and was taken off. On January 26 of the following year (1612) Hawkins followed, having apparently taken Jourdain's advice. But he outwitted his wife's relatives in an amusing way. He persuaded the Jesuits to make him out duplicate passports, one an open one licensing him to settle down as a trader in Goa, the other a secret permit to return to England, 'and what agreements I made with them to be void and of none effect, but I should stay and go when I pleased.' What marginal notes on 'Jesuiticall Sanctitie' would a similar procedure on the part of his opponents have evoked from the worthy Purchas!

SURAT THE FORT FROM THE RIVER BRIDGE

Hawkins, his wife, and the other Englishman, were taken on board under an armed escort, Mukarrab Khan, overawed by the Portuguese fleet, peremptorily refusing to allow a factory to be opened or any English traders to be left behind at Surat. Before starting, Middleton made a most valuable discovery, acting on information supplied by Jourdain from native sources.[1] This was the location of the famous Swally Hole, a fine roadstead seven miles long and a mile broad, protected from the sea by a long sandbar. Here a fleet could ride at anchor much more safely than among the shifting shoals of the Tapti. Swally became the port of Surat and acquired great fame.[2] Otherwise Middleton had accomplished nothing during a stay of 138 days. On his way out he had been robbed and imprisoned by the Arabs at Mocha, and he was burning for revenge. Accordingly his fleet weighed anchor and sailed along the coast to Dabul, destroying Portuguese shipping, and then crossed over to Aden and blockaded the mouth of the Red Sea. Many Mohammedan ships were held up for ransom, including the huge *Rahimi*, a pilgrim ship belonging to the Queen Mother, which paid 15,000 reals of eight. The blockade was spoilt by the arrival of Captain John Saris with the Eighth Voyage; as usual, the rival commanders could not agree, and unfortunate squabbles about precedence rendered co-operation between the two fleets impossible. On October 19, 1612, they set sail for Tiku in Sumatra, where, in the following January, Hawkins and his wife took a passage on the *Thomas*, homeward bound. They reached Saldania Road on April 2, and here Hawkins's diary ends. He 'dyed on the Irish shore',[3] no doubt, like so many of the adventurers of his time, of disease contracted in the East.

Finch, who had started by the overland route after having been badly treated, if Jourdain is to be believed,[4] by Hawkins,

[1] Hawkins, refusing to give his enemy any credit, says that Middleton discovered Swally 'miraculously', 'and never known to any of the country'.

[2] 'The Road of Swally and the Port of Surat are fittest for you in all the Moghal's country. . . . The Road of Swally is as safe as a pond' (Roe, *apud* Foster, ii. 345).

[3] Purchas, *Pilgrimage* (1626 ed.), p. 521.

[4] Journal, p. 157.

died at Bagdad. Middleton went on to Bantam, and on the way the *Trade* ran on to a coral reef and was much damaged. While she was being careened for repairs, she was fired and destroyed by the Javanese.[1] 'It was a ship of eleven hundred tons, for beauty, burthen, strength, and sufficiency, surpassing all merchants ships whatsoever,' laments a contemporary. 'But alas, she was but shewn; out of a cruel destiny she was overtaken with an untimely death in her youth and strength.'[2] Middleton, disheartened by the 'tired, crost, and decayed voyage', turned his face to the wall and died, 'most of heartsore', say the old records. One hundred and forty of his crew quickly followed him. The rest were found by Jourdain, 'like ghosts or men frighted', and 'scarce able to go on their legs'. Downton struggled home in the *Peppercorne*, his men dying like flies of scurvy and his timbers strained and leaking. But he had a rich cargo of spices, and the Sixth Voyage, for all its disasters, paid over 121 per cent. in dividends. Of him, as of Mrs. Hawkins, we shall hear anon. Jourdain was murdered in 1616 by the Dutch off Patani. They shot him on his own quarter-deck after he had hauled down his flag.

Hawkins's mission was, directly, a failure. He had failed to obtain from Jahangir even the worthless *farmans* he bestowed upon other English ambassadors. Jahangir, convinced by the Jesuit Fathers that the English were a paltry and distant race who wanted to rob him of his trade, took no notice of him when he had exhausted his stock of novelties and good stories. The English are only once mentioned in that monarch's voluminous memoirs.[3] Nor was any change likely to come about while the Portuguese fleet could blockade the coast at will. A decisive victory at sea was supremely

[1] Peyton's Journal in Purchas, *Pilgrimes*, iv. 304. The dangers of voyaging in those days were great, and the casualties in men and ships were terrible. Besides the *Ascension*, *Union*, and *Trades Increase*, the *Darling*, *Thomasine*, *Hector*, and *Hosiander*, were all lost before 1616; Middleton, Hawkins, Downton, Aldworth, and a host of sailors, died of disease, to say nothing of casualties in men and ships in engagements with the Portuguese and Dutch.

[2] Quoted in Anderson, *English in Western India*, pp. 17–18.

[3] A casual reference to the battle of Swally Hole (Rogers and Beveridge's transl., i. 274–5).

necessary for English prestige. But indirectly the results were very important. Hawkins had thoroughly explored the resources of the Mughal Empire (of which he wrote a very able account) and had investigated the possibilities of Surat as the site for a factory. He may not unfairly claim to be ranked among the founders of the Indian Empire.

CHAPTER IV

THE STRUGGLE WITH THE PORTUGUESE BY SEA, 1612–35

HAWKINS left Surat in February 1612. The next Englishman to put into the port was Captain Thomas Best with the Tenth Voyage, which consisted of the *Dragon* and the *Hosiander*.[1] They cast anchor off the Bar on September 5, and were met by Jadav, Hawkins's old broker. Thomas Kerridge was sent ashore and received a hearty welcome from the Governor, who was no doubt overawed by Middleton's peremptory dealings with his opponents; but he brought back a letter which Sir Henry had left with the Mukadam of Swally, warning them of possible dangers ahead. The warning came none too soon, for on the 13th sixteen Portuguese 'frigates'[2] appeared, and made prisoners Mr. Canning the purser and another Englishman who had landed. Best replied by putting a prize crew on board a large Gujarat ship anchored near him, and seizing ten of the crew as hostages. He then moved his fleet out of the Tapti round to Swally Road, where there was more sea-room in case of an attack, especially by light craft. Here the Governor of Ahmedabad, who was probably desirous of standing on good terms with both sides, came to visit him. Best went ashore to greet him, still keeping his hostages on board. He then drew up thirteen 'Articles of Trade' with the Governor, of which the principal were:

1. Compensation for the attack on Sir Henry Middleton and a promise not to repeat the offence.

2. The King was to receive a permanent English Envoy at Agra.

[1] Captain Best's own narrative in Purchas, iv. 119. The *Hosiander* is described by Purchas as 'a little Ship, scarcely a ship, I had almost called her a little pinnasse'.

[2] Light galleys, mounting a gun in the bows, used for river and coastal work. They usually had about twenty soldiers aboard and eighteen oars on each side.

TAPTI RIVER FROM THE PRINCESS GARDENS SURAT

3. The arrival of each English Fleet was to be publicly proclaimed, and the country people to be allowed to trade freely with it.

4. Customs duty not to exceed three and a half per cent., and cartage from Swally to Surat to be provided by the Mukadam at a fixed rate. Provisions up to 1,000 dollars to be sold to ships without duty.

5. If an Englishman died, his effects were to be invoiced and returned intact.[1]

6. The Mughal authorities were to be responsible for any molestation on the part of the Portuguese in their territory.

7. The English Company was not to be held responsible for the misdeeds of pirates and interlopers, though it would do its best to suppress them.

8. Speedy redress was to be given for wrongs and injuries.

9. The articles of the treaty were to be confirmed by the Royal Seal.

Best refused to send the King any present until the treaty was signed. Just then Canning came on board with news that a Portuguese fleet was comingfrom Goa,[2] and sure enough, on November 29, four great galleons and from twenty to thirty frigates hove in sight, under the command of Admiral Nunes d'Ancunha. The Portuguese (as well they might, from their enormous superiority in ships) showed their usual arrogance, assuring the Surat officials that they would 'force us to yield in an hour'.[3] Best weighed anchor and stood out to meet them, but found himself alone, the *Hosiander* having fouled her cable. Nothing daunted, however, after a few words to the crew, he laid the old *Dragon* two cables' length off the enemy (he was unable to close owing to shoal water), and, to continue the story in his own words,

'began to play upon the Vice Admiral both with great and small shot, that by an hour we had well peppered him with

[1] The goods of an alien dying in Mughal territory were liable to confiscation to the Government. This was a constant source of friction.

[2] 'Master Canning had been taken by the Portugals but the viceroy commanded to set him ashore at Surat, saying, "Let him go help his countrymen to fight, and then we will take their ship and the rest of them altogether".' (Narrative of Nicholas Withington in Purchas, iv. 163–4).

[3] Narrative of the Rev. Patrick Copland, in Purchas, iv. 148–9.

some fifty-six great shot. From him we received one small shot, saker or minion, into our mainmast, and with another he sunk our longboat: now being night we anchored, and saved our boat but lost many things out of it. The thirtieth, as soon as the day gave light, I set sail and steered between them, bestirring ourselves with our best endeavours, putting three of their four ships on the sands thwart of the Bar of Surat.'

The next morning the battle was renewed, and the *Hosiander*, making up for her inaction on the previous day, 'danced the hay upon them,[1] so that they durst not show a man above the hatches'.[2]

'At nine I anchored', continues Best. 'This morning the *Hosiander* did good service, and came through also between the ships and anchored by me; upon the flood the three ships on ground came off: we set sail, they at anchor, and came to them, and spent upon three of them one hundred and fifty great shot: and in the morning, some fifty shot: and at night, we giving the Admiral our four pieces out of the stern for a farewell, he gave us one of his prow pieces, either a whole or a demi-culverin, which came even with the top of our forecastle, shot through our davy, killed one man, to wit, William Burrell, and shot the arm of another. This day the *Hosiander* spent wholly upon one of the ships which was on ground, and from the enemy received many shot, one of which killed the boatswain Richard Barker. Night being come, we berthed ourselves some six miles from them and anchored: and at nine of the clock they sent a frigate to us, which being come near, came driving right on the half of the *Hosiander*: and being discovered by their good watch they made to shoot at it: the first caused it to set sail: the second went through their sails and so they took their leave. Their purpose, doubtless, was to have fixed us, if they found us without good watch.'[3]

Best now held a council of war, and as the bay was shallow and the *Dragon* drew much water, decided to run up the

[1] 'Hey or Hay', an Elizabethan round dance in the figure of eight. '*Dull*. I'll make one in a dance, or so; or I will play on a tabor to the Worthies, and let them dance the hay' (*Love's Labour's Lost*, Act V, Scene i).

[2] Withington, *op. cit.*, p. 164. Withington's narrative shows some minor discrepancies from Best's. He also by a slip dates the battle October 29.

[3] Purchas had it from 'Mr. Salmon the actor' that the frigate was sunk and eighty men drowned.

coast. Here they anchored off 'Mendafrobay,[1] where all that time Sardar Cham,[2] a great nobleman of the Mogolls, with two thousand horse was besieging a Castle of the Razbooches [3] (which were before the Mogoll's conquest the nobles of that country, now living by robbery'. This was on the Kathiawar coast, about ten leagues east of Diu, and Sardar Khan and Best exchanged compliments and presents. This was a splendid chance to show the Mughals the mettle of English seamen, and as luck would have it, 'after ten days stay here, the Portuguese, having refreshed, came hither to our ships. Sardar Cham counselled to flee: but the General chased the Portugals in four hours, driving them out of sight before thousands of the country people; Sardar Cham relating this to the King (after the Castle razed) to his admiration, which thought none like the Portugals at sea'.[4] This fight, which did much to enhance our prestige and proportionately lower that of the Portuguese, was fought on December 23–4. By the 27th Best was back in Swally. He had only lost three sailors in action, while the enemy's casualties had been very heavy—at least 160 killed. The *Dragon* had fired 680 'great shot', 3,000 'small shot', and 60 barrels of powder. On February 6 the royal *farman* arrived, and Best refused to receive it unless it was formally delivered. Unfortunately, it was hardly worth the paper on which it was written. 'The articles agreed upon by Captain Best were never signed by the king otherwise than in a general *farman* without knowledge of particulars, and are of small validity', writes Kerridge to Roe in 1615.[5] On February 17 he hoisted sail for Bantam. He passed the Portuguese fleet as he sailed down the coast, but they did not fire, and allowed him to take a vessel under their very eyes.[6] Disgusted at the perfidy of the native officials, and seeing the difficulty of

[1] Muzafarabad or Jafarabad on the Kathiawar coast thirty miles east of Diu. (Not Mahuva.) See Map, p. 91.

[2] Sardar Khan, or Khwāja Yādgār (Blochmann, *Ain*, p. 492; Rogers and Beveridge, Jahangir's *Memoirs*, i. 237; ii. 89).

[3] Rajputs, who often took to the hills as highwaymen, 'a kind of *tories*' as Mandelslo puts it. See p. 108, *infra*.

[4] Withington's narrative, *op. cit.*

[5] *Embassy of Sir. Thos. Roe*, ed. Foster, i. 62 n.

[6] Purchas, iv. 133–4.

protecting the interests of the factory from their insults and the attacks of the Portuguese during the interval which must necessarily elapse between the departure of one fleet and the arrival of the next, Best had at first been inclined to abandon Surat altogether.[1] He was, however, dissuaded from this course by Thomas Aldworth, who was, accordingly, left in charge, together with his relative, Thomas Kerridge, Withington, Starkey, and others. Canning, in accordance with the terms of Best's treaty, went up to Agra as the Company's agent to present the letter from James I. Jahangir at first received him well, but when he found out from the Jesuits that he was a mere merchant and not sent immediately from the King of England, he contemptuously referred him to Mukarrab Khan. Canning was treated with studied neglect; his servants deserted him, and he went in constant fear of poison. On June 22 he died, and Purchas assumes that the Jesuits made away with him.[2] Kerridge, an honest, capable, though hot-tempered man, and a good linguist, took his place. It was, however, impossible to effect much in the face of the unwearied opposition of the Jesuit Mission, headed by Jerome Xavier, the implacable enemy of the English. 'We shall never do anything, as long as that witch Xavier liveth', writes Withington.[3] This proved to be correct, but fortunately, Xavier died a few years later, and was succeeded by the courteous and tolerant Father Corsi.[4]

Meanwhile, it was decided to send Withington on a tour through Gujarat, to report upon the trade of the country, especially as regards indigo. He was accordingly 'entertained factor and bound to the Company in four hundred

[1] *Letters Received*, ii. 157. According to Kerridge, Best quarrelled with Aldworth on the subject, but afterwards took all the credit for the latter's action.

[2] Withington's narrative, Purchas, iv. 165; and Dodsworth's narrative, *ibid*, p. 257. See also *Letters Received*, vol. ii. (1613–15), which does not support the story that Canning was poisoned.

[3] *Embassy of Sir Thos. Roe*, ed. Foster, ii. 313 n.

[4] Terry, *Voyage* (1777 ed.), p. 422–3. Corsi was 'a man of severe life yet of a fair and affable disposition'. He asked Roe that there might be 'a fair correspondence between them but no difference . . . that Christ might not seem by those differences to be divided among men professing Christianity'. He offered him 'all good offices of love and service'.

pounds'. In the cold weather he travelled through Broach, Baroda, and Ahmedabad, as far as Tatta in Sind. Here his escort turned upon him and robbed him. He was kept a prisoner for three weeks, after which he escaped, stripped and penniless, to Ahmedabad. Withington notes that in the course of his travels he encountered many 'fugitives and renegades', English and German (mostly deserters who had fled their ships to avoid punishment), who had turned Muhammadan and settled in the country.[1] At Surat, the factory was maintained by the devoted labours of the heroic Aldworth; time after time, the native officials, 'but for his persuasions would have again received the Portuguese'.[2] Anthony Starkey, whom he dispatched overland with letters to the Company, died on the way—'poisoned by two friars', says Purchas.[3] The only other Englishman of note at Surat was Richard Steele, an amusing adventurer with a fertile imagination, who had been sent by the Company to Persia on one of the many attempts made to recover some of the goods embezzled by Mildenhall, and had brought Aldworth a glowing account of the country and its prospects.

An unusually favourable opportunity for opening relations with the Mughal court now presented itself. The Portuguese had bitterly offended the Mughals by plundering the *Hassanie*, a Surat ship bound for Jeddah, carrying £100,000 worth of treasure, and by making marauding expeditions down the coast, burning Gogo on the way.[4] Jahangir was furious. He banished 'Xavier the great Jesuit' from court, shut up the church at Agra, and told Mukarrab Khan to attack Daman.

'Had we now English shipping here', writes Aldworth, 'we might do great good in matter of trade, which is now debarred to people of this country, having none to deal with them. They all here much wish for the coming of our English ships, not only for trade but to help them, for as they say, the coming of our ships will much daunt the Portugals.'[5]

[1] Withington's narrative, Purchas, iv. 170 ff.
[2] *Letters Received*, II. xxi.
[3] Purchas, iv. 133, marginal note.
[4] Downton in Purchas, iv. 215 (A.D. 1614).
[5] Aldworth to the Company, August 19, 1614 (*Letters Received*, ii. 96–7).

Under these circumstances, the factors were prepared to give a warm welcome to the fine fleet which anchored in Swally Road on October 15, 1614. This was the Second Voyage of the First Joint Stock, commanded by Captain Downton. The squadron consisted of the *New Year's Gift*, flagship, of 650 tons; the old *Hector*, of 500 tons; the *Merchant's Hope*, of 300 tons; and the *Solomon* (named after the 'British Solomon'), of 200 tons. 'It hath pleased God to send hither in safety four gallant ships from the worshipful Company, and four hundred gallant men in them, which is no small joy to us', writes Aldworth to Kerridge, in high spirits, his anxious and weary vigil at last at an end.

Downton was determined to assert his authority. He landed with great pomp, and placated Mukarrab Khan's rapacity with a number of novel presents, well suited to the childish humour of the recipient. These included, we are informed, cases of knives and combs, pictures of Moses and of Paris in Judgement, and last, but not least, sundry cases of bottles of 'rich and strong waters'. Mukarrab Khan was very anxious that Downton should employ his fine fleet in combined operations against Diu, and was very sulky when that prudent captain replied that he would not be hired to fight against the Portugals, 'which is contrary to my King's Commission[1] (unless they gave me first cause), not for the world; neither would I be witheld from fighting with them if they provoked me'.[2] The factory at Surat was now overhauled. Aldworth was left in charge at his own request. Edwards was sent up to Agra to present a letter from James I to Jahangir, together with some pictures of the Royal Family, a case of strong waters and an English mastiff. Dodsworth was sent to Ahmedabad to start buying indigo; Steele and Crowther were dispatched to Persia, to investigate the question of trade with that country. News now came that the Portuguese, enraged at the arrival of a fresh English fleet, were preparing a formidable armada to crush them once and for all, whereupon Mukarrab Khan, alarmed for the safety of

[1] Given in *First Letterbook*, pp. 449–52. He was not to attack any Christian allies of the King of England unless 'by them first justly provoked'.

[2] Downton, *op. cit.*, p. 219.

Surat, began to be more civil. On December 23, the anniversary of Best's glorious fight, Portuguese scouting frigates appeared up the Tapti; this continued over Christmas, and shots were exchanged, after which Downton put out to Swally Road. Here, on January 18, 1615, the Portuguese armada arrived—six great galleons, the largest of 800 tons, three other ships, sixty frigates, and two galleys; altogether they mounted 234 guns, with 2,600 European, and 6,000 native sailors, against Downton's 400 men and 80 guns.[1] In command was no less a person than the Viceroy of the Indies, Don Jeronimo de Azevedo, himself. The natives were overawed by this overwhelming display of force, and Mukarrab Khan, thinking defeat for the English was inevitable, began to negotiate with the presumed victors. Downton realized the gravity of the situation.

'My care is not small', he wrote, 'how to do my best in maintaining the Honour of my Country, nor negligent in the memory of the estates and charge of my friends and employers in this journey; not only for the hazard of this at present committed to my charge, but also all hope of future times, if I should now be overthrown: by reason the enemy, in getting the upper hand of me, would make his peace with these people upon what conditions he lust, to the expelling of our Nation this country for ever.'

The odds were, indeed, terrible.

'The Captain was furnished with abundance of all things the country might yield and wanted nothing but an upright cause, fit for God to favour. He came to the place where he found what he sought—four poor merchant ships and a few men, and many of them sick and dead.'[2]

One asset, however, Downton had, which was worth all the guns in the Portuguese armada.

'The thing with me to give me hope was my people (though

[1] GALLEONS: Viceroy on the *All Saints*, 800 tons, 300 men, 28 guns, all brass; *St. Benet*, Captain M. de Souza, 150 men and 20 guns, 700 tons; *St. Lawrence*, Captain J. Cayatho, 600 tons, 160 men, 18 guns; *St. Christopher*, 600 tons, 160 men, 18 guns; *St. Jeronymo*, 180 men, 500 tons, 16 guns; *St. Anthonio*, 400 tons, 140 men, 14 guns. SHIPS: three, 200 tons and 8 guns each. GALLIES: two of 50 men each. FRIGATES: sixty, 18 oars a side, and 20 soldiers in each. Dodsworth's account (taken from a Portuguese prisoner) in Purchas, iv. 263. Cf. Aldworth in *Letters Received*, ii. 137; Low, *History of the Indian Navy* (1877), i. 19.

[2] *Ibid.*, p. 249.

much with death and sickness shortened), all from the highest to the lowest seem very courageous and comfortable.'

After much thought and silent prayer, Downton decided that it was useless to waste more time. The enemy must be brought to battle. He therefore called a council of officers on his ship and found them all 'to my heart's desire and tractable to whatsoever I would wish'.

Unfortunately, Downton's abilities as a tactician were not equal to his honesty and good-will. He was only a gallant amateur, and his men were not trained gunners, though their pieces were excellent. He himself had never really recovered his nerve after the terrible experiences of the homeward voyage in the *Peppercorne*. He ought, like Best, to have gone out into the open where his superior seamanship might tell, instead of being 'besieged in a fish pond', as Roe puts it.[1] He decided to anchor the *Hope*, under Captain Molineux, at some distance from the rest of his fleet, in order to tempt the Portuguese to attack in shoal water. He apparently overlooked the danger of separating his small command in the face of overwhelming odds and forgot that the enemy was well provided with river-craft. 'I put forward the business as it were, baited my hook, and the fish presently ran thereat.' The Portuguese attacked the *Hope* in force, so suddenly that Downton (who was in his cabin writing his diary) had to cut his cables in order to come to the rescue in time. 'They came three ships and thirty or forty frigates as I imagined', he writes, 'with a veaze laid the *Hope* aboard with the flower of all their gallants: where by the hand of God in their amazed carriage they received such a blow as few (and they by their extraordinary chance) escaped with safety, and three ships burnt.' The attack was within an ace of succeeding; but after a desperate struggle the boarders were hurled into the sea, where those who had not been shot or drowned were picked up by the Portuguese light craft. 'The *Gift* in this fatal month', cries Purchas exultingly, 'answered her

[1] He acknowledges his mistake in a subsequent letter to the Company: 'If the Portugals had not fallen into an error at the first, they might have destroyed the *Hope*, and by likelihood the rest, hastening to her aid.' (*Letters Received*, ii. 186.)

name and gave them for a New Year's Gift such orations (*rorations* I may call them), that they were easily persuaded to leave the *Hope*, and all hopeless, to cool their hot blood by leaping into the sea's cool waters.'[1] This bombast contrasts rather disadvantageously with Downton's own sober remarks. 'I never see men fight with greater resolution than the Portugals', he confesses, 'therefore not to be taxed with cowardice as some have done. The gallants of the Portugal's army were in this business.'[2] The three frigates which had grappled the *Hope* were set adrift, having first been fired by the English sailors, 'doubting what trains might be left aboard'. And sure enough, after drifting on to the shoals, they blew up 'in a fearful manner'.

After this the fight dwindled into an inconclusive cannonade across the bank. The *Hope* again suffered severely. A man, armed with explosives and 'wildfire' to throw into the enemy's rigging, had been stationed in the maintop. He received a bullet which caused him to drop a match into his own combustibles; a fire ensued, and the mast was destroyed. Every morning and evening the English fired a salvo into the enemy, hoping to provoke him to attack; and the natives, seeing how the fight was going, began to bring them fruit and stores, and articles of commerce such as indigo, bastas, and cotton. At this time Downton suffered a grievous blow to add to his other anxieties.

'It pleased God', he writes, 'this day at night, when I had least leisure to mourn, to call to His Mercy my only son George Downton, who early the next morning was buried ashore, and the volleys aforesaid, appointed to try the temper of the Viceroy, served also to honour his burial.'

News came from Daman that the Portuguese had buried 300 corpses there. On the 5th and 8th, attempts to destroy the fleet by fireships were again foiled by the watchfulness and good shooting of the English fleet, and then the Viceroy shifted his fleet down the coast so as to threaten Surat. But Downton prepared to attack him the moment that he commenced to disembark his force, and soon after the Portuguese

[1] *Pilgrimage* (1626), p. 527. [2] *Letters Received*, ii. 186.

admiral, having run out of food and water, stood out to sea and disappeared. Downton's fleet was crippled by the loss of the *Hope's* mainmast, and as a prudent merchant he did not wish to imperil the Company's ships, and so did not pursue.

> 'I wish no occasion to fight', he notes, 'for that which I have already paid for I am already possessed on, and I am so far from the humour to fight for honour, unless for the Honour of my King and Country, that I had rather save the life or lives of one of my poorest people than kill a thousand enemies.'

There was much rejoicing ashore at the defeat of the Portuguese. Downton and the Nawab exchanged swords and paid one another complimentary visits. On March 3, the fleet weighed anchor for Bantam; the Viceroy's fleet appeared on the horizon and followed Downton down the coast, but did not dare to attack. Downton's achievement had been indeed a notable one.

> 'Though they beleaguered us round about by sea with all their sorts of ships for many days together, our people still in actions and half tired with continual labour, some receiving in goods; yet, blessed be God, they could never get the advantage to win from us the value of a louse, unless our bullets which we lent them, his fireboats failing and nothing prospering; and once in four and twenty hours I sent him a defiance for many days together to try his temper; all which must needs lie heavy on the stomach of a gentleman of so great courage.'

It is sad to learn that this gallant captain soon after died at Bantam, the fatal climate of which had undermined the health of Middleton, Hawkins, and vast numbers of merchants of lesser note.

> 'He dying in this voyage and following his son', says Purchas, 'hath left this glorious act, *Memoriae Sacrum*, the memorable epitaph of his worth, savouring of a true heroic disposition, piety and valour being in him seasoned with gravity and modesty. We will not with heathen poets cry out of cruel immature fates; for Death hath prevented unto him possibility of disastrous events (which as shadows follow bodies in greatest light) and leaving his living memory here, hath lifted his lively part and virtuous spirit to receive the

applause and praise and reward of God and with God, to whom be glory for ever. Amen.'

The Portuguese power in the East was now on the downward path. In 1615, Captain Benjamin Joseph's fleet, with Parson Terry aboard, encountered off Madagascar a great Goa carrack commanded by Don Emmanuel de Menezes. 'She was a ship of exceeding great bulk and burthen, our *Charles*, though a ship of 1,000 tons, looking like a pinnace when she was beside her', says Terry.[1] Don Emmanuel gallantly refused to surrender when challenged, and kept up a running fight, hanging out a lantern at night lest his pursuer should miss him. The battle was a severe one, Captain Joseph being killed and his successor, Captain Pepwell, severely wounded. Finally the Portuguese commander, having lost his mainmast, beached his ship on the island of Comoro and burnt her. This victory not only damaged Portuguese prestige, but put Goa itself in jeopardy, for it demonstrated that communications with Portugal were in danger of being cut. 'She was very rich, and the succour of India this year', says Roe. 'This is the greatest disaster and disgrace ever befell them, for they never missed their fleet in September, nor lost any such vessel as this, which was esteemed invincible; and without supplies they perish utterly.'[2] Keeling's fleet, in the same year, put the Portuguese to another test. On their way to the Far East they anchored unopposed at Calicut and made a treaty with the Zamorin. At Crangalor they landed George Wolman with five men and a boy, to start a factory. At Coulan they captured a Portuguese vessel from Bengal under the Castle walls. So low had the once mighty Viceroy of Goa now fallen.[3] Five years later, the Company's fleet under Captain Andrew Shilling, flagship the *London* of 800 tons,[4] engaged off Jask a formidable Portuguese armada, dispatched from Goa under the gallant Ruy Frere de Andrade, the Pride of Portugal as the factors called him,[5] 'our avowed enemy',

[1] *Voyage* (1777 ed.), pp. 34–47.
[2] *Journal of Sir Thos. Roe*, ed. Foster, ii. 359.
[3] Narrative of Walter Peyton in Purchas, iv. 298.
[4] The other vessels were *Roebuck*, *Hart*, and *Eagle*.
[5] *English Factories*, 1618–21, p. 228.

who had 'taken the Sacrament in Portugal to ruin both us and our trade in these parts'.[1] The Portuguese had two galleons, one bigger than Shilling's flagship, two Flemish ships, two galliats and ten frigates. Contact with the enemy was made on December 17, when the English tried to send in a fireship, but failed.[2] After a fierce cannonade, in which the *Roebuck* was hit and the Portuguese lost their vice-admiral and about forty men, the English ran into Jask and safely landed their cargo, which was taken over by Monnox. A period of fruitless manœuvring followed, the English being baffled by light breezes and contrary winds, so that the natives 'after their heathenish superstition were persuaded that the Portingalls had brought with them from Ormus a witch to bring them continually a fair wind'. Meanwhile, Ruy Frere played the part of Fabius Cunctator, exasperating his opponents by 'domineering, with music, flags and pendants'.[3] At last, on December 28, 'about nine of the clock, the Lord sending us a pretty eastern gale, our fleet weighed and put all things in order for fight'. The wind dropped again when the enemy were within range, when the English anchored and

'the great ordnance from our whole fleet played so fast upon them, that doubtless, if the knowledge in our people had been answerable to their willing minds and ready resolutions, not one of these galleons, unless their sides were impenetrable, had escaped us. About three of the clock in the afternoon, unwilling after so hot a dinner to receive the like supper, they cut their cables and drove with the tide (then setting westerly) until they were without reach of our guns; and then their frigates came up to them and towed them away, wonderfully mangled and torn; for their admiral in the greatest fury of the fight was inforced to heeld his ship to stop his leaks, his maintopmast overboard and the head of his mainmast. The greater Fleming both his topmasts and part of his bowsprit shot away. The lesser Fleming never a shroud standing, never a topmast.'

The English followed all night, but being short of ammuni-

[1] *English Factories*, 1622–3, p. 33.

[2] Richard Swan's account in *English Factories*, 1618–21, p. 220 ff.

[3] His idea was apparently to draw the English into shoal water or get them separated.

tion did not attack again. They had won a decisive victory, and were enabled to trade in the Persian Gulf without interference. The English losses were incredibly small—three killed and five wounded. Unfortunately, among the latter was the gallant Shilling, who 'in the beginning of our second fight received a great and grievous wound through his left shoulder by a great shot, which hurt he with such courage and patience underwent, that gave great hope to us all of his most wished recovery'. But it was not to be. On the 5th he was very ill, and desired his shipmates to pray for him. He 'remained valiant, and spake cheerful, with thankfulness to God, the last minute of his life', and at noon on January 6 he passed to his rest, 'shewing himself, as ever before a resolute commander, so now in his passage through the gates of death a most willing, humble, constant and assured Christian'. So died another of the stout merchant-seamen who gave their lives for the Company in these distant seas. His comrades buried him at Jask, and the fleet returned to Surat.

In 1621, the English, emboldened by this striking success, determined to take the offensive. The key of the Gulf was the frowning citadel of Ormuz.[1] Shah Abbas, enraged at Portuguese pretensions, had attacked the town from the land side, but was unable to make progress while the sea lay open. Monnox, the chief of the English factory in Persia, was eager that the Company's ships should co-operate, and Weddell and Blyth, with a fleet of five ships, arrived off Jask at the psychological moment. They took the bold step of joining hands with the Persian commandant, and immediately set to work. In the meanwhile, an Anglo-Dutch fleet blockaded Goa and prevented the Portuguese from sending reinforcements. Ormuz was protected by the fortified island of Kishm, and this the English first attacked. Ruy Frere, who was in command at Kishm, tried hard to make terms, but as the allies insisted on an unconditional surrender, he refused to betray his Persian troops to the tender mercies of their fellow-

[1] For the siege of Ormuz, see *English Factories*, 1622–3, *passim*, and map therein. Herbert's account is given in the appendix to this chapter.

countrymen, and resolved to fight it out. Kishm fell after a fierce bombardment, in which Baffin, the famous Arctic explorer, lost his life.[1] Ruy Frere and the rest of the garrison were put on board the *Lion* and taken off in triumph to Surat. But the English had not yet done with their gallant opponent. One dark night he plied the sentries with drugged wine, and escaped in a skiff, to the intense chagrin of the factors.[2]

Meanwhile, the fortress of Ormuz was fiercely assailed by land and sea, and fell on April 23. The Portuguese garrison, with their women and children, were taken off by the English fleet; the Persians found in the town were put to the sword by their countrymen. The fall of this proud bulwark of the Portuguese power in the East re-echoed all over the world. It struck their prestige a deadly blow, from which they never recovered. Assailed by the Dutch on the one hand and the English on the other, Goa was doomed. Nevertheless, though impoverished by misgovernment and corruption, and paralysed by Spanish neglect at home, our rivals put up a determined fight. In the autumn of 1625 the English fleet under Captain Weddell on the *James* arrived at Swally with the veteran Kerridge aboard, to find four Dutch ships about to sail for the Persian Gulf. As the Portuguese were blockading Ormuz and causing much damage to trade, it was decided to combine the squadrons for an attack upon them. On January 31 they encountered a strong Portuguese fleet under Nuno Alvarez Botelho. Kerridge stepped on to the deck of the flagship and drank to the men, 'encouraging all of them to perform with alacrity and boldness that committed to their charge, solemnly protesting, for our better encouragement, that if it pleased God we overcame our enemies (of which he made no doubt), the pillage taken should be equally and without partiality divided among all men, share and share alike, without the least giving accompt thereof to any man breathing under the cope of heaven'. 'The bare name of pillage', the anonymous writer quaintly continues, 'did so animate our men

[1] He was master of the *London*. While sighting a gun he received a bullet in the stomach, 'wherewith he gave three leaps and died immediately' (Purchas, ii. 1792).

[2] *Op. cit.*, p. 83.

that at that instant they severally promised to use their best endeavours, come life, come death!'[1] The fight was long and fierce, the sailors fighting 'as though it had been a May game', 'courageously cheering with a hubbub, shouting, whistling and stirring in their several places'.

'The fight continued as bloody as it was at the first . . . it cannot be but we killed them many men; the durance of the fight was such a thing as it is thought to be one of the greatest that ever was fought, the sea being all as calm and smooth as the Thames, and we continually board by board. But about six o'clock in the evening the enemy withdrew themselves from us, and we wanting cartridges (having not above a hundred left) were willing to give over for that night.'[2]

So ended a notable engagement. But Botelho was not yet at the end of his resources. He suddenly appeared off Swally, and nailed to the doors of Surat Castle, where all men might see it, a challenge to the English to come out and fight again. When the Anglo-Dutch fleet, nothing loath, put out to sea in response to the invitation, they found that they had been tricked. Botelho had sailed southward with all speed, and next made his presence known by pouncing upon the outward bound fleet. Half of them he chased northwards to the Persian Gulf, where Ruy Frere was waiting to co-operate with him. They waylaid and boarded the *Lion*, the fine vessel which had brought out Sir Thomas Roe, and burnt her to the water's edge under the very walls of Ormuz Castle. Botelho now once more disappeared. Word, however, came to the English authorities that he had 'got into a hole called Bombay, where they were fitting themselves up for the war, and look for three more ships from Goa to join forces with them'.[3] To Bombay, accordingly, hastened the Anglo-Dutch fleet, hoping to catch Botelho before he effected a junction with his reinforcements. But once more they found that the birds had flown. However, they were not to be baulked of their revenge. Bombay under the Portuguese was a flourishing port, inferior indeed to Goa, but equipped with storehouses, docks, and the usual complement of monasteries and churches.

[1] *English Factories*, 1624–9, p. 46.
[2] *Ibid.*, pp. 51–3.
[3] Captain Weddell's report (*ibid.*, p. 112).

A landing party 'left the great house, which was both a warehouse, a friary, and a fort, all afire, burning with many other good houses, together with two new frigates not yet from the stocks'. This was on October 15, 1626—a historic date, as it marks the first landing of the English forces at a spot which their descendants were destined to make famous.[1] A strange story is related of the end of Botelho. During the sack of Bombay a Dutch captain pillaged the church of Our Lady of Pity, tearing down the crucifix and smashing it. Botelho on his return swore an oath never to rest until he had chastised the wretched iconoclast, and hung a piece of the sacred symbol round his neck as a reminder. And sure enough, shortly afterwards he perished in an engagement with a Dutch vessel; his opponent was also slain, and the legend goes that he was none other than the man for whom Botelho was seeking.

Desultory fighting went on till 1630, in which year Captain Morton repeated Downton's exploit by frustrating a landing of the Portuguese at Swally. This little engagement made a great impression on the natives, and the place where the invaders were repulsed was long after known as Bloody Point.[2] Both sides were now tired of a war which brought no profit to either, and the English were beginning to doubt the wisdom of an alliance with the Dutch. A truce, which afterwards developed into a regular treaty, brought the long and fruitless struggle to an end in 1633.

APPENDIX TO CHAPTER IV

THE SIEGE OF ORMUZ

THIS famous siege, which heralded the downfall of the Portuguese power in Asia, is described in many contemporary and subsequent books of travel. I select for reproduction the picturesque account given in Herbert, *Travels* (1665 edition, p. 115), as it is well told, though inaccurate in some details.

'By command of *Shaw Abbas*, *Emangoly-chawn*[3] (Governour

[1] *English Factories*, 1624–9, p. 112.

[2] *Ibid.*, 1630–3, pp. ix, x; see also Fryer's *New Account*, ed. Crooke, i. 224.

[3] Imam Quli Khan.

of those Territories that extend from *Shyraz* unto the gulph of Persia,) advances towards *Gombrown*[1] with nine thousand Horse and Foot, such a time as he expected to meet the English Fleet there. Being met, the Conditions betwixt them under Hand and Seal were these: 1. That the Castle of *Ormus*, (in case it were won) with all the Ordnance and Ammunition should belong unto the *English*. 2. That the *Persians* might build another castle in the Isle at their own cost, and where they pleased. 3. That the spoil should be equally divided. 4. That the Christian prisoners be disposed by the *English*, the Pagans by the *Persians*. 5. That the *Persians* should allow for half-charge of victuals, wages, shott, powder &c. 6. That the English should be Custome-free in *Bander-gorm-broon* for ever. These articles being signed, each party prepared for fight.

'Captains of note in the Pagan army under the Duke of *Shyraz* were *Alliculy bey*, *Pollotbeg*, *Shakulibeg*, *Shareearee*, *Mahomet Sultan*, and *Alybeg* King (*Shawbander* they call him) of the Port: These with the Army first encamped before *Bander-gom-broon*; and two days after, *viz.* the twentieth of *January* 1622, with small difficulty became Masters of the Port; for at that time it had in it but a small garrison of *Portugals* in an inconsiderable Fort. After which success the Duke and English Captains played upon the Castle with a dozen pieces of Cannon for five hours, but to little purpose. The ninth of *February* the *English* transported three thousand *Persians* in two Frigots which they had lately taken, and two hundred Persian boats which were good for little other service: These, so soon as they landed, having formerly made Sconces for their men, and raised Bulwarks to plant great Ordnance upon, made towards *Ormus*; but the *Portugal* though they let them land, stopped the current of their fury, at first encounter from their barricadoes defended with shot and pike slaying above three hundred, and with their Ordnance beat them back with more haste and amazedness than their approach had courage. In this disorder a Flanker by mischance was blown up, but the siege continued. Little hurt was done on either side till the 24 of *February*; when the *English* advanced towards the Castle (under which was riding the Portugal Armado) and in despight of the Castle and Fleet (being then five Gallions and twenty Frigots) set fire on their Admiral the Saint *Pedro*, a ship of one thousand five hundred

[1] See the map in *English Factories*, 1622–3. Gombroon (Bunder Abbas) is on the mainland; Ormuz, Sarak, and Kishm are islands at a short distance from it.

Tun; Which mischance observed, the rest of the Spanish Fleet to prevent more danger cut her cables, and in that flaming posture let her drive whither wind and tide would. The *English* were well pleased with that sad sight; and though a prize rich enough, nevertheless thought it not safe to adventure boarding; so down she drove towards *Larac*, in the way a rabble of *Arabians* and *Persians* boarding her, and like Jackalls with hunger-starved fury and avarice tearing her asunder. The seventeenth of *March* the *Persians* (to shew they were not idle) gave fire to a Mine stuffed with forty barrels of powder, which blew up a great part of the wall, doing some harm to the Enemy; through which breach the *Portugals* immediately sallied, and maintained a fight above one hour against the *Persians*, who had drawn out all their body; and when the trumpets sounded, the besieger went on so couragiously, that the hindmost discovered plainly a contempt of death. After nine hours the defendants were forced to retreat, and the heated *Persians* began to mount and enter the city in many quarters; at which the Portugals were glad; for they entertained them with so many hand-grenadoes, fire-balls, powder-pots and scalding lead, that the assailants were forced to fall back, a thousand of their men perishing; which when *Shaculibeg* had viewed, with a party of two hundred men he passed through those affrighting fires, and after a short storm scaled one of their Flankers; which he held not above half an hour, they were so tormented with small shott, and flames of lead and sulphur; and in descending were beaten off by fifty Huydalgoes, who for three hours maintained their ground, and retreated gallantly. This entertainment so cooled the *Persians* courage, that for five days they did nothing but ruminate upon the valour of their adversaries. The three and twentieth day our Cannon from the shore played so hotly, and battered their Fortifications so to purpose, that at length making the ships their object, they sank the Vice and Rear-Admiral of *Ru-Fryero's* Fleet. *March* the twenty eighth necessity humbled them (plague, famine and fluxes raging in the City) so as five days after two Gentlemen in a fair equipage first made towards the Enemies camp. [Here follows an account of abortive negotiations between the Portuguese, Persians, and English.] Two days after a hideous noise of thunder amazed them, the *English* giving fire to two several mines, so as the breach gave an open prospect into the City; but the hearts of the assailants durst not travel with their sight, their senses the last time were so confounded; so that they onely became spectators, and gave new courage to the *Portugals*, most of whom were half dead with fluxes and thirst (the three great cisterns of the City being exhausted) famine and pestilence. The fourteenth day a ship full of Mulettoes from *Kishmy* arrived at *Ormus* to help the *Portugals*; but perceiving it impossible to approach with safety, they turned back, thinking to land at some better quarter; But the Persian General assuring them they should receive no detriment from his Army, they foolishly gave credit to it, till fourscore of their heads being struck off, and the rest in chains, made the survivors see their folly.

'The *Ormuzians* languishing thus under many afflictions, every hour hoped for *Ru-Fryero* to raise the siege, but he failed their expectations. The seventeenth day another breach was made by giving fire to sixty barrels of powder, which took such effect that the Moors entered in swarms, who yet were beaten back by eighteen Gentlemen without the bulwark; howbeit, next day the Infidels re-entred and possessed it. The eighteenth of *April* two famished renegadoes stole into the Persian camp, and discovered to the Duke the sickly condition of the City, and the little defence the besieged were able to make; that gave the *Persian* fresh encouragement upon the next opportunity to make a general storm. [Here follows an account of the treacherous massacre and plunder of the city by the Persians: the heroism of the Portuguese contrasts strongly with the cowardice and cruelty of our allies.]

'After the sack of this City, the Sea-men found enough to throw away, by that little they got shewing their luxury; nothing but *Alea, Vina, Venus*, appearing in the ascendant of their devotion. Captain *Woodcock's* luck was best and worst; for by chance he lighted upon a Frigot that was stealing away laden [1] with above a million of Ryals, (as some say if their multiplication deceive them not,[2]) the most of which he presumed came to his own share: But alas! what joy had he in that fading pelf? For whether *Woodcock* minded more his Mammon than the steerage of his ship, who can tell? but many by sad experience found that the *Whale* sunk close by *Swally-barr*, the name neither of bird nor fish availing against that merciless element, which is a good Servant but a bad Master, and then yielded neither

[1] *v.l.* 'loden with pearls and inestimable treasure'.

[2] No doubt an exaggeration. The Spanish ambassador said that the *London* took £500,000 worth of spoil! (*Letters Received*, 1622–3, p. xii. *note*.)

safety nor comfort. Such was the *exit* of this famous City, after the *Portugals* had been Masters of it six-score years, or thereabouts.'

NOTE ON AUTHORITIES

For Best's fight we have (i) *A Journal of the Tenth Voyage to East India . . . written by Thomas Best*; (ii) *Certain observations written by others employed in the same voyage, Master Copland Minister, Robert Boner Master, Nicholas Withington Merchant* (Purchas, iv. 119–75).

For Downton, (i) *Extracts of the Journal of Captain Nicholas Downton . . . wherein is related their happy success against the Vice-roy and all Indian sea forces of the Portugals, by force and cunning attempting their destruction*; (ii) *Relations of Master Elkington and Master Dodsworth, touching the former voyage* (*Ibid.*, pp. 214–66).

Other sources of information are his letter (*Letters Received*, ii. 185); those of Elkington, Mallory, and Squire (*ibid.*, iii. 7, 44, 48) with Foster's illuminating criticism; and that of Aldworth (*First Letter Book*, p. 437) and his commission (*ibid.*, p. 449).

For the Battle of Jask, see Richard Swan's narrative in Purchas, v. 241, reprinted in *English Factories*, 1618–21, p. 220 ff., with other accounts, also additional authorities quoted in foot-note.

For the Siege of Ormuz, see *English Factories*, 1622–3, introduction and map, and authorities quoted in foot-note to p. xi. (Herbert's account is given above.)

For the later operations, see *English Factories*, 1624–9, and 1630–3, and authorities quoted therein.

CHAPTER V

THE EMBASSY OF SIR THOMAS ROE, 1615–18

At first it appeared as if Downton's success had greatly altered the prospects of the English in Western India. The Surat authorities seemed inclined to relax the harassing restrictions which they had hitherto imposed. Branch factories were started at Cambay, Broach, Baroda, Ahmedabad, and Agra, and the Company's agents went as far as Lahore and Sind. Edwards, thanks chiefly to his opportune present to the royal menagerie of a mastiff which 'pincht' a young leopard to death and tackled a wild boar, was affably received by Jahangir, who gave him a worthless *farman* and a present of 3,000 rupees. Edwards began to give himself mighty airs in consequence; his head was quite turned; he posed as an ambassador, and treated with scorn both Kerridge and Aldworth. The former had stayed on at Agra to act as his 'linguist' or interpreter, but found himself relegated to the background, and even accused of purposely delaying an answer to James I's letter. 'Mr. Edwards in his carriage here seemeth absolute,' writes Kerridge, 'for he conferreth not of any business publicly, nor will hear of any counsels.' On a proposal being made to sell certain remainders worth £10,000 at Surat, Edwards wrote that 'Mr. Aldworth should do nothing without his order, which if he withstood, he would let him know his strength'. Contrary to the Company's rules he kept Jahangir's present, and spent it on riotous living. 'For Mr. Edwards,' complains Downton to Smythe, 'I never see cause to like neither his carriage nor his husbandry, yet I conceited his pride to be such as to spur him on to work much at Court, and that was the best construction I could make when I consented to his going thither: but since, his unfit and imperious carriage to his companions, and his plotting for great and vainglorious expense puts me into an extraordinary doubt.'[1] Edwards retorted that Downton was an ungodly fellow who neglected his prayers and stayed away from church; he wasted time on the voyage out, and bullied to death poor young Henry Smythe, a relative of the Governor's who had come out in the Company's service. It might be expected that the presence of a minister of religion would calm the atmosphere, but the Reverend Peter Rogers, the Company's chaplain, joined hotly in the fray. He reproved Downton for his many shortcomings, and found him 'much given to backbiting'. The much-harassed Commander, we are not altogether surprised to hear, 'answered my fatherly remonstrances by saying scornfully that he could tell his duty better than I could advise him, and such like demonstrations of pride and hypocrisy.'

Edwards appears to have led a faction in the factory. Later on, his absurd conduct at Agra led to his dismissal. He was 'ordered by the General[2] and his Council to repair to Surat, to answer unto certain objections exhibited against him by the greatest part of the English factors in the Great Mughal's dominions, whereto he not giving sufficient satisfaction, was by the joint consent of the Governor and his Council ordered to take a passage for England in the *Lion*'.[3] This roused the wrath of Joseph Salbanke, a worthy and religious minded factor, who had several grievances of his own as well. Salbanke had carried himself 'very genteelly' to Keeling, but had been forced to work under 'punies and younglings' who might have passed for his grandchildren.[4] Salbanke wrote to the Company very strongly in Edwards's favour.

'Needs must the arrogant General Keeling call Mr. Edwards from the place where he remained at the King's Court and summon him by the thunderbolt of his threats to come before him: whither no sooner did he repair, but immediately some of them, like a company of cruel vultures, seized upon him with their cruel gripes, laying hands not only upon his goods, which in their great wisdom forsooth they confiscated to the use of your Right Worshipful Company, and also many other

[1] Downton to Smythe, February 28, 1615, in *Letters Received*, iii. 27. *Vide* also pp. 14, 72–83, and 89.

[2] Captain Keeling.

[3] Letter of the Factors to the Company, March 10, 1616.

[4] Anderson, *English in Western India*, p. 20.

discourtesies unbeseeming his place and quality, which I, that was no seer but only a hearer of such unsupportable wrongs offered to so worthy a person, did not a little condole his misery. I think I may boldly affirm that neither before his time hath been nor now is his peer of an Englishman to be found in this country for merchandize affairs.'[1]

Bickerings like these fill the records of the period. The anxious life got upon the nerves of the factors. Their position was not enviable. The climate was trying to people who had not yet learned how to adapt themselves to Eastern ways of life. The mortality was high, and between the departure of one fleet and the arrival of the next, which occurred at totally uncertain intervals, they were practically cut off from the outer world. They were harassed by the avarice and caprice of the native officials and by the constant menace of the Portuguese. All things considered, Aldworth's task was not an enviable one. Added to his other anxieties, was the friction, sometimes threatening serious results, caused by unruly and drunken sailors and others, ignorant of native prejudices. Thus, the English love of beef gave great offence to the 'Banyans', who paid the Muhammadans an annual sum to stop cow-killing. A curious sailor peeps into a litter containing a *purdah* lady: a page boy pokes his finger into a Brahmin's food! Parson Terry has an amusing tale of a cook who got drunk, and swaggering down the street, met the Governor's brother and his attendants.[2] 'Now, thou heathen dog!' he cried, and accompanied his words with a blow from his sheathed sword. The astonished nobleman had the offender arrested, but magnanimously pardoned him. A serious riot broke out over another trifle which nearly cost Kerridge his life. A small belfry had been erected outside the English factory, surmounted by a vane. The mob attacked the building, declaring that the vane was a cross, 'a sign of victory and winning the town', and the bell a 'watchword to give the alarm', and it was only with the greatest difficulty that they were pacified.

The prospects of the English now received a rude shock.

[1] *Letters Received*, iv. 231. [2] *Voyage* (1777 ed.), p. 163.

Jahangir, as capricious as ever, tired of them when they had no more presents to offer, and turned once more to the Portuguese. Edwards had been found out, and like Canning before him, fell into disgrace. He ' had suffered blows of the porters, base *peons*, and been thrust out by them with much scorn by head and shoulders without seeking satisfaction ', which had ' bred a low reputation of our nation '. Kerridge himself had been beaten and fined by the authorities at Ahmedabad, owing to some dispute about indigo. Worst of all, Jahangir now proceeded to hand over the charge of Surat to the haughty Prince Khurram. Khurram himself hated foreigners, and left the transaction of his business to his favourite, Zulfikar Khan, who was no better disposed to the English than had been the last Viceroy, Mukarrab Khan. A treaty was actually being negotiated by the latter with the Viceroy of Goa for the landing of a Portuguese force at Swally to expel the English from Surat and permanently exclude them from the country.[1]

It was, then, plain that something had to be done, especially as the Dutch were threatening at the same time to drive us out of the Malay Archipelago. Fortunately the matter had already been taken in hand, and the Company had decided to accept the advice of its factors and send out a representative who should really be an ambassador, and who should ' breed regard ' in the Mughal Court. James I was quite agreeable to this. Like Elizabeth, he affected an interest in the enterprise of the Company, and had frequently furnished its merchants with letters of introduction to Eastern monarchs. In 1609 he had been present with the Royal Family at the launching of the unlucky *Trades Increase.* Hence he readily acquiesced in the project of sending Sir Thomas Roe as his representative to the Mughal Court, with instructions to act as the official representative of the English nation in order to obtain a permanent treaty with the Mughal monarch, authorizing the opening of factories on the coast and at other places of commercial importance.

Sir Thomas Roe, who appears to have been selected by

[1] *Embassy of Sir Thos. Roe*, ed. Foster, i. 95, n. 2.

Sir Thomas Smythe, was eminently suited for the post. He belonged to an old City family, and was able to sympathize with the Company's mercantile aspirations. He had sat as Member of Parliament for Tamworth. He had already been on an important voyage to South America and up the Amazon. However, he was at first regarded by some members of the Company with suspicion. They disliked 'gentlemen', and they were afraid that the king might foist on them some courtier who would pry into their profits,[1] and perhaps try to overthrow their coveted monopoly. It was only when Sir Thomas, by his tact and firmness alike in dealing with the native authorities and the unruly English factors, and by his excellent advice on the subject of reorganizing the Company's factories, had shown how much he had their interest at heart, that they really took him into their confidence. 'My Lord Ambassador hath managed his place very honorably since he came to the Moghal's Court,' wrote Salbanke, 'with that frugal respect of your profit that I believe you could hardly have picked out a fitter and worthier man for the administering of his place in our whole kingdom.'

The agreement drawn up between Roe and the Company is instructive.[2] The Governor and Company have nominated him, and procured His Majesty to employ him as his ambassador to the Grand Mughal for the better establishing and settling an absolute trade in the dominions of that monarch. Sir Thomas is to keep a strict account of all his expenses, and to deduct from them any allowance made by the Grand Mughal. He promises not to engage in private trade, directly or indirectly, and to report to the Company any offenders whom he shall detect infringing this rule. He is on no account to meddle with the Company's investments or moneys in India, but to leave them entirely to the management of the local factors, and he is not to ask for an advance of over £100. On their part, the Company is to pay Sir Thomas £600

[1] When the English took Ormuz, the Company had to give the King and Buckingham £10,000 each. 'Did I deliver you from the complaint of the Spaniard and you return me nothing?' asked the former.

[2] *Embassy of Sir Thos. Roe*, ii. 547 ff. The Company's *instructions* are missing.

per annum, half to be invested in the Company's stock, with £100 for servants' wages, £100 to buy plate for his table (to be returned when the contract ends), a preacher at £50, and a surgeon at £25 per annum.

The King's Commission to Roe,[1] after stating that the object of his mission was 'to maintain the intercourse and traffic which hath so happily been begun', gave him full powers and authority to treat with the Great Mughal and his representatives at his discretion, 'concerning the maintainance and continuance of the amity and course of merchandize between us, our realms and dominions, and the realms and dominions of the said Great Mughal.' In the event of his being unable to negotiate a treaty with the Mughal Empire, Roe might be employed in exploring the Red Sea or any other places likely to be of service. The Commission concludes with the usual caution against fighting with Spain or any other nation at peace with England, except in defence of his rights. In the private instructions issued to Roe, James exhorts him 'in his carriage to be careful of the preservation of Our honour and dignity', and to do all he can to advance the Company's interests and to carry out their instructions. If the Great Mughal asks him why, in spite of the peace with Spain the Viceroy of Goa still attacks the English, he is to explain that the Portuguese 'desirous to engross to themselves the whole trade and commerce of those parts of the East Indies', 'do seek to deprive Our subjects from that liberty of commerce in those parts which the Law of Nations doth cast upon us'. In order to remove the bad impression about the English spread by the Portuguese, he is to dwell upon 'the quality and constitution of Our Estate, as well in regard of the several kingdoms and people which Almighty God hath subjected unto us, as in those other blessings which God hath bestowed upon Us and Our hopeful posterity'. Above all, he is to extol 'Our power and strength at Sea, which giveth Us not only reputation and authority amongst the greatest princes of Christendom, but maketh Us even a terror to all other nations'.

[1] *Embassy*, ii. 550.

Roe sailed with the Third Voyage of the First Joint Stock. It was a noble fleet. The flagship, the *Lion*, was commanded by the veteran Captain Keeling, General of the voyage, the other vessels being the *Dragon*, the *Peppercorne*, and the *Expedition*. They set sail on January 24, 1615, and reached Swally on September 18. The voyage was a dull one, especially for Roe, who was looked on with some suspicion as an outsider who wanted to interfere in the Company's affairs. At the Cape they met the *Hope*, with news of Downton's victory and death. On September 27 Roe landed at Swally Hole with a salute of forty-eight guns, the fleet being decorated with 'ensigns, flags, pendants and streamers'. He was, however, rudely received by Zulfikar Khan, who wished to search him and his servants and overhaul his goods at the Customs House. Roe politely but firmly refused to submit to this violation of the privileges of an ambassador, and plainly intimated that he intended to be treated with respect. A month was passed in weary wrangling with rapacious officials, whose manifest object was to extract presents, after which Roe determined to wash his hands of them and to go straight to Agra and lay his case before Jahangir himself. Meanwhile, the Company had received a serious blow. The heroic Aldworth, who was lying desperately ill at Ahmedabad, 'more like an anatomy than a man,' tried hard to come down to meet Roe. But he died at Nadiad, a few miles outside that town, on October 4. 'All is now ended, and I destitute and distressed for want of so dear a friend,' writes Kerridge, who tried in vain to get his body removed to Ahmedabad and buried under a decent tomb, 'that some memory may be of him to succeeding times.'

Roe and his party set out for Agra on November 1. They halted at Burhanpur, then an important fort and the headquarters of Prince Parviz, who made it the base for his operations in the Deccan. Here Roe obtained permission to establish an English factory, and sat down to indite to the Company an account of his progress up to date.[1] He begins

[1] *Ibid.*, i. 93 ff.

by pointing out the deplorable position of the English at Surat. 'First, for the liberty of your people, I found them all in absolute servitude, so as no private man, much less a nation, could endure.' 'I was esteemed an imposture like my predecessors; two before having taken the title of Ambassador, Master Hawkins and Master Edwards, but so that they have almost made it ridiculous to come under that quality.' The Portuguese were still in bad odour at Court, though a strong party, including Mukarrab Khan and Prince Khurram, were trying to negotiate a treaty with them for the expulsion of the English from Mughal territory. Roe recommended a vigorous offensive as 'the nobler and safer part', and the most likely to impress the natives. He was inclined at the time to think Surat a bad port for a fleet likely to be attacked, and recommended Muzaffarabad, on the opposite coast of Kathiawar, as a possible alternative; but this opinion he subsequently retracted.[1] He urged the opening of trading stations on the Indus, at Jask, and on the Bengal coast. Roe went on to point out that the parsimony of the Company about presents (burning glasses, telescopes, tawdry pictures and knives, a case of virginals, and a coach, the cheap velvet lining of which had faded on the voyage) had made him utterly discredited, and urged that the unworthy suspicion and secrecy with which he was received by the factors made it impossible for him to examine the state of their finances or offer any further advice.

Roe arrived at Ajmere on December 23, but he had contracted a severe attack of fever on the road, and remained prostrate until January 10, when he was admitted to the royal presence. The courtiers in vain tried to induce him to make the oriental *salaam*, touching his forehead upon the ground. Roe refused to do anything of the kind. He had long seen that it was necessary to uphold above all things

[1] It is interesting to note that Salbanke was impressed by the courtesy of Mahabat Khan as compared to the 'cruel griping' Governor of Surat, and wanted to take the port of Broach 'where we may safely land all our goods whatsoever, faithfully promising that we should be absolutely exempted from all such exactions and injuries as we were subject unto in Surat' (*Letters Received*, iv. 233).

English prestige, and to insist upon being treated with the respect due to the ambassador of a great nation. He accordingly walked straight up to the inner railing reserved for the highest nobles, and stepped in. He bowed to the emperor, who returned the salute. He then, to the horror of the court, demanded a chair. 'I was answered', says Roe, 'that no man ever sat in that place, but I was desired as a courtesy to ease myself against a pillar covered with silver that held up his canopy'. Jahangir then asked him what he wanted, whereupon Roe explained the injuries practised upon the English traders, and asked permission for a factory in the town. Jahangir, his eye no doubt upon the English coach and other presents, ordered a *farman* to be drawn up, but upon reading it, Roe found that he was asked in return to allow the Portuguese to come and go as they liked in and out of Surat harbour. After some complicated diplomacy, which may be best enjoyed in Roe's own delightful pages, our ambassador presented a draft of the treaty he wished to conclude with Jahangir, the following being the chief clauses it contained: [1]

1. Permission to come and go freely into any Indian port, to land goods, and to hire a house and establish a factory there.

2. Facilities to be afforded for trade with the inhabitants in provisions, and labour and cartage to be provided.

3. Goods landed at any port not to be tampered with at the Custom-house; presents for the King not to be pilfered or opened; and merchants not to be searched or otherwise insulted on landing.

4. Goods to be sold freely to any one, and at any price, after dues are paid; no presents to be exacted, or unnecessary escorts imposed; and sealed packages brought from inland not to be reopened.

5. The Portuguese must either make peace with the English and agree to free and open trade at Indian ports, or in case of refusal it shall be lawful for the latter to 'chastise the stubbornness of an obstinate enemy to Peace, as also to

[1] *Embassy*, i. 152 ff.

requite any robberies made by them, in taking any of their ships, boats, or goods'.

More delays of course occurred over this document, as Prince Khurram, an enemy to all Europeans except the 'Portugals', demurred at the last clause. He even asked Jahangir why he favoured the English, who only gave mean presents such as knives and cloth, instead of the Portuguese with their rubies, pearls, and other costly gifts? The Prince consented, however, to grant *farmans* restricting the local governors from robbing and oppressing the factors at Surat and Ahmedabad. Shortly after this the Portuguese arrived with a 'Balass Ruby'[1] weighing five ounces; worse still, a Dutch deputation from Surat also appeared, and was granted the same privileges as the English.

The months dragged on wearily. At one time Roe was debarred the Court, but by Jahangir's birthday he was back again, amusing the King with miniatures and himself an amused spectator of the intrigues of nobles and courtiers. About this time Roe finally learnt that the King would not sign the treaty, and he had to be content with a *farman* from Prince Khurram, authorizing the English to trade in peace at Surat. In the following month the English fleet arrived with Parson Terry on board, bearing the news of their victory over the Portuguese galleon off the Comoro Isles; Sir Thomas made the most of this, and the Portuguese were correspondingly depressed; but little came of it from the King beyond an inquiry about novelties in the way of presents.

In November, Roe again wrote home to the Company.[2] After some general remarks about his progress in the first year, he retracts his former doubts about the suitability of Surat as a port of trade, tapping as it does the rich country of Gujarat, but is strongly averse from any projects of building a fort or maintaining any armed force. 'A war and traffic are incompatible', and the Portuguese and Dutch have ruined themselves in this way; all that is required is a light pinnace of say sixty tons and ten guns to keep off the

[1] A ruby-coloured spinelle, found in Badakhshān.
[2] *Embassy*, ed. Foster, ii. 342.

enemy's frigates. At sea, on the other hand, Roe always advocated a forward policy. The Portuguese were on the downward grade, and a blockade of Goa, by cutting them off from the annual home-fleet, would quickly bring them to their senses and make them agree not to molest our traffic.[1]

As regards trade, Roe did not recommend the opening of fresh factories, either in Bengal or at the mouth of the Indus. 'They will increase charge but not recompense it.' Nor was Roe now very eager to start trading with Persia, and here he thought the factors at Surat had behaved very badly to him. The idea of opening up trade with Persia dated from 1608, when the Shah had sent Sir Robert Shirley[2] to Europe to open negotiations with the European governments. Shirley returned to Persia in 1613 with Sir Thomas Powell as ambassador from King James. The party came to a disastrous end; Sir Thomas died, and the same fate befell his brother Michael and his wife, who perished with her new-born infant, after an affray on the Indus which, no doubt, frightened the poor lady with fatal results. Richard Steele, however, had journeyed overland to India through Persia, and had persuaded the factors to send him and one Crowder on a mission to the Shah. They reached Ispahan, and reported upon their success to Aldworth. Aldworth being dead, Roe opened the letter and answered it, which so angered Kerridge and his companions that without telling Roe or taking his advice, they sent Connock in the *James* to start trading with Jask at once. Roe himself was much more eager to open trade with the Red Sea, which he thought offered much greater prospects of profit for the Company.[3]

[1] This was the policy subsequently adopted, with satisfactory results, by the English and Dutch fleets.

[2] The Shirleys (or Sherleys), Robert and Anthony, were gentleman adventurers who had been employed by Shah Abbas in organizing his army. Robert married a Persian wife who created a sensation in London. After his return to Persia in 1615, he was again sent to Europe on a prolonged mission; but presenting himself once more at the Persian Court in 1628, he was told he was no longer required. He died shortly afterwards, and his body was taken by his wife and buried at Rome.

[3] Here the merchants were right, and Roe was mistaken. The silk trade, inaugurated by Connock, was a most valuable asset, which subsequently saved the Surat Factory from bankruptcy.

Roe ends his letter by pointing out the futility of his mission as an ambassador. It was impossible to obtain a regular treaty: Jahangir could not be brought to treat with the King of England as an equal, and all that could be obtained was a few trading concessions and *farmans*. These, however, Roe considered sufficient for the purpose: meanwhile he thought that all that the English required at the Court was a native consul at 1,000 rupees a year to represent the interests of the English, with a subordinate at Surat on half this sum. That, said Roe, 'will serve you better than ten ambassadors'.

In the cold weather of 1616 the Court moved to Mandu, Roe and his suite with it, and an amusing example of Jahangir's childish rapacity was given when the presents under the charge of Terry arrived at the royal camp. The King, unable to wait for the donor's arrival, opened the boxes and purloined the contents, even down to some 'beaver hats' intended for Roe's private wear.[1] The hot weather and rains of 1617 passed away, and still nothing was done. Roe was wearily waiting for his recall, when at the end of September arrived the Company's fleet of five vessels, commanded by Captain Pring on the *Royal James*.[2] Second in command was the gallant Captain Shilling on the *Anne*. Great was Roe's joy, and he addressed Pring as the 'welcomest man to this country that could arrive to assist my many troubles'. Pring, however, brought an urgent request to Roe to stay for another year, with which the latter reluctantly complied. The *Bee*, one of Pring's vessels, was dispatched to Persia in accordance with the Company's orders. The fleet brought out some unusual passengers to India. These were our old friend Mrs. Hawkins, her companion Mrs. Hudson, and her maid Frances Webb. With them were Richard Steele, and Mr. Golding, a chaplain engaged by the Company. Mrs. Hawkins, after the death of her first husband, had consoled herself by marrying Captain Gabriel Towerson, the master of

[1] For Jahangir's childish love of toys, cf. Covert's remark: 'I gave him a small whistle of gold, weighing almost an ounce, set with sparks of rubies, which he took, and whistled therewith *almost an hour*.'

[2] The other ships were the *New Year's Gift*, the *Bull*, and the *Bee*. On the way they took a Portuguese vessel and two English 'interlopers trading for the Earl of Warwick.

the *Hector*, Hawkins's old ship. She was a rich woman, for when she and Hawkins had left Agra, she had taken with her diamonds to the value of £6,000, no doubt procured for her by her step-father, Abraham de Duyts, Prince Khurram's court jeweller. To this the Company had added a sum of 200 Jacobuses,[1] 'as a token of their love'. On the way out Steele got into trouble with Frances, and the pair were wedded 'under a tree', at the Cape. A baby (the first English baby born in Surat) arrived soon after they landed. Mrs. Towerson and her party went straight up to Agra, where she no doubt hoped to derive a rich profit from private trade with her Armenian relations. Golding, who was very fond of the ladies, instead of attending to his duties at Surat, followed them disguised in 'Moor's apparel'.[2] Roe disliked them all. He had Golding arrested for unclerical behaviour. Of Steele he had already formed a low opinion from his exaggerated reports to the Company about the Persian trade, which he characterized as 'contradictory and silly, magnifying his own works'. How he dealt with them all may be best judged from what he wrote to the Company on the subject:

'I found him (Steele) high in his conceits, having somewhat forgotten me, Master Kerridge and him at wars, which I endeavoured to temper on all parts; but for his wife I dealt with him clearly, she could not stay with our safety nor his masters' content; that he had ruined his fortunes if by amends he repaired it not; that she should not travel nor live on the Company's purse; I know the charge of women, that if he were content to live himself like a merchant, as others did, frugally, and to be ordered for the Company's service and to send home his wife, he was welcome; otherwise I must take a course with both, against my nature. Having to this persuaded him, I likewise practised the discouragement of Captain Towerson about his wife (you know not the danger, the trouble, the inconvenience of granting these liberties); to effect this, I persuaded Abraham, his Father-in-law here, to hold fast; I wrote to them the gripings of this Court, the small hope of relief from his alliance, who expected great matters from him.' [3]

[1] A gold coin of James I, worth twenty-five shillings.
[2] *English Factories*, 1618–21, p. 32.
[3] *Embassy*, ed. Foster, ii. 478.

Accordingly, Gabriel Towerson let his wife return to her own people, while he went to the Far East to take charge of the English factory at Amboyna. Here he and the other factors were barbarously murdered, after nameless tortures, by the Dutch in 1623. Mrs. Towerson, not unnaturally, objected strongly to this treatment, and as late as 1627 she was still 'railing' at the Company, after having vainly endeavoured to extract a sum of 220 rupees from Kerridge.[1] Steele was an amusing ne'er-do-well; we hear subsequently of his hare-brained schemes for water-works at Agra, on the model of those at London. After his return to England he was not sent again to India.[2]

In February 1618, Roe sat down to write his last report to the Company, though neither this nor his letter to Sir Thomas Smythe adds very much to what he had already told them. He warns his employers to give up hope of a regular treaty between the two nations, and bids them be content with general *farmans* obtained from time to time when necessary. He sees no real impediment in the way of English progress: the Portuguese are on the downward path, and as for the Mughals, 'their justice is generally good to strangers: they are not rigorous, except in searching for things to please'. He promises before leaving to obtain as much as he can, and this promise he was fortunately able to redeem by a clever piece of diplomacy. Steele had smuggled up country a famous pearl 'shaped like a pear, beautiful and orient!' Roe promised to sell this to Asaf Khan, Hawkins's old friend. Asaf Khan was the brother of the Empress Nur Mahal, and had quarrelled with Prince Khurram. He therefore willingly championed Roe's cause in return for the jewel, and obtained for the English a final *farman* far more favourable than anything he had previously received. The local authorities were to protect the English if attacked by the Portuguese: free trade was to be allowed, and the factor's goods were not to be detained or plundered at the custom-house: the factors were to live under their own laws and religion, and were to

[1] See, e.g., *English Factories*, 1618–21, pp. 169, 327, &c.

[2] He was given a post at Bantam in 1626, and was dismissed for private trading.

be allowed to lease a house for their factory, though not to buy or build one: and in case of any violation of the foregoing articles by any one, the Governor of Surat was to 'aid and entreat them as friends, with courtesy and honour'.[1]

In August, Roe had a narrow escape. Plague had broken out in Ahmedabad, and many of his suite died of it.[2] But his work was now finished, and in the following month he shook the dust of the Court from his feet for the last time. Returning to Surat, he enjoyed a four months' well-earned rest in a pleasant country villa in the suburbs of the town, and it is comforting to note that the factors, who had fiercely opposed him at first as a prying intruder, now acknowledged his good sense and integrity. In February 1619 he sailed on the *Anne* with Towerson and the Steeles, and arrived in England in September. He was greeted with an ovation: the Company voted him £1,500, and the King received him at Hampton Court. He afterwards served as ambassador at Constantinople, Hamburg, and Vienna, and died—it is said, broken-hearted by the Civil War—in 1644.

Roe's visit is the turning-point in the history of the British in Western India. He did not, it is true, obtain a definite treaty, for a formal agreement of this kind was alien to the nature of the capricious and indolent monarch, and in any case would have been a 'scrap of paper' to the holders.

'The privileges which he sought', Kerridge writes rather spitefully to the Company, 'were ever denied in capitulations, the custom of other princes. His Lordship at departure had only two several *farmans*, one of the king and another of the prince, confirming our trade and continuance; the king's, general, for our reception and free trade in all his dominions: the prince's, more particularly prohibiting wrong and injustice, hath coldly reformed it, as may appear as well by the detention of our goods as their not providing us a fitting house.'[3]

But from Roe's time we find the English treated with respect, and what is more, replacing the Portuguese by steady steps as the paramount foreign power in the Mughal's

[1] *Embassy*, ii. 506 ff.

[2] Plague first appeared in the Panjab in 1616 and raged for eight years (V. A. Smith, *Oxford History of India*, pp. 381–2).

[3] *English Factories*, 1618–21, p. 59.

dominions. Terry aptly compares Roe to Joseph in the Court of Pharaoh, winning favours for his brethren, and certainly the letters of Jahangir to James I, of which translations are given by the chaplain,[1] are, even after allowance has been made for Oriental hyperbole, a landmark in the relations between England and India. Not the least valuable result of Roe's visit was the advice which he was able to give the Company about the conduct of its internal affairs, a task which he carried out with consummate delicacy and tact; and his reports upon the trade of India, Persia, and the Red Sea were of the utmost assistance in directing their policy. The Company was indeed well served, and Roe could justly write to his employers, 'my sincerity toward you in all actions is without spot: my neglect of private gain is without example, and my frugality beyond your expectation'.[2]

[1] *Voyage* (1777 ed.), pp. 415–17. [2] *Embassy*, ii. 343.

CHAPTER VI

THE EARLY DAYS OF THE FACTORY AT SURAT, 1618–33

EARLY in 1619, Roe had sailed for England, leaving the Surat factory in the capable hands of Kerridge, who now informally assumed the title of President. Of the latter years of Kerridge's incumbency not much remains to be told, and we may perhaps be pardoned for devoting a page to the story of some of the visitors to Surat at this time, as described in the lively pages of Parson Terry, Roe's genial chaplain. Surat, the great port of call of the Mughal Empire, saw many visitors from western lands, all of whom found a ready welcome at the hospitable English factory. None, however, was stranger than crazy Tom Coryat, wit, linguist, and buffoon, who arrived at Agra in 1616, after wandering over Egypt, Turkey, Palestine, and Persia. He was born at Odcombe in Somerset, and before his latest excursion, had tramped over half Europe, and had recorded his wanderings in a strange medly which he entitled *Coryat's crudities, hastily gobbled up in five years' travels in France, Italy, &c.*, and to which Ben Jonson contributed some introductory verses. Many stories are told of his adventures in India. He had a marvellous gift of tongues, and on his arrival at Agra, delivered an oration before Jahangir, in which he compared himself to the Queen of Sheba and that monarch to Solomon. Jahangir contemptuously tossed him a purse of one hundred rupees. Roe, who was there at the time, was furious at this buffoonery, which lowered the prestige of the English in the eyes of the Court, and he expressed his feelings in no uncertain terms to Tom; 'but', says our wanderer, quite unabashed, 'I answered him in that stout and resolute manner that he ceased nibling at me!'

On another occasion he talked down a loquacious washerwoman, the terror of Roe's *entourage*, completely silencing her by eight in the morning! But his most remarkable feat was to mount an eminence at the time when the call to prayer was sounding from a neigbouring minaret, and, parodying the *muezzin*, to proclaim *La alah, ala alah, Hazrat Isa Banala*—there is no God but God, and Jesus the Son of God! On this occasion he only escaped with his life because he was looked upon as a lunatic, and religious maniacs in the East are regarded with superstitious reverence.[1] Vanity was not the least of Tom's failings, and he was elated to hear from Steele that James I had asked after him; but when he was told that the king's actual words were *Is that fool yet living?* 'it seemed to trouble him very much, because he spake no more nor no better of him; saying, that kings would speak of poor men as they pleased'. Not less was his mortification when Roe, in writing him a letter of introduction to the factory at Aleppo, spoke of him as an 'honest poor wretch'. Coryat's end was pathetic enough. He travelled to Surat, though he was suffering from a severe attack of dysentery; 'but being over kindly used by some of the English who gave him sack which they had brought from England, he calling for it as soon as he heard of it and crying "*Sack, sack*, is there any such thing as *Sack*? I pray you give me some *sack*"; and drinking of it, though I conceive moderately (for he was a very temperate man) it increased his Flux which he had then upon him; and this caused him, within a few days after his very tedious and troublesome travels (for he went most on foot) at this place to come to his journey's end; for here he overtook death in the month of December 1617, and was buried under a little monument like one of those usually made in our churchyards'. As Fryer says, 'he was killed with kindness by the English merchants, which laid his rambling brains at rest'. Fryer,[2] following Herbert,[3] says he was buried at Surat, 'on a small hill on the left hand of the road', outside the present Broach Gate. Terry, however, declares that he rests 'at the East Indian Shore at Swally, on the banks thereof', and as he was a contemporary and personal friend of Coryat's, he is probably correct.

[1] He was known as the 'English Fakir', says Fryer.

[2] *New Account*, ed. Crooke, i. 253.

[3] *Travels*, 1665 ed., p. 43.

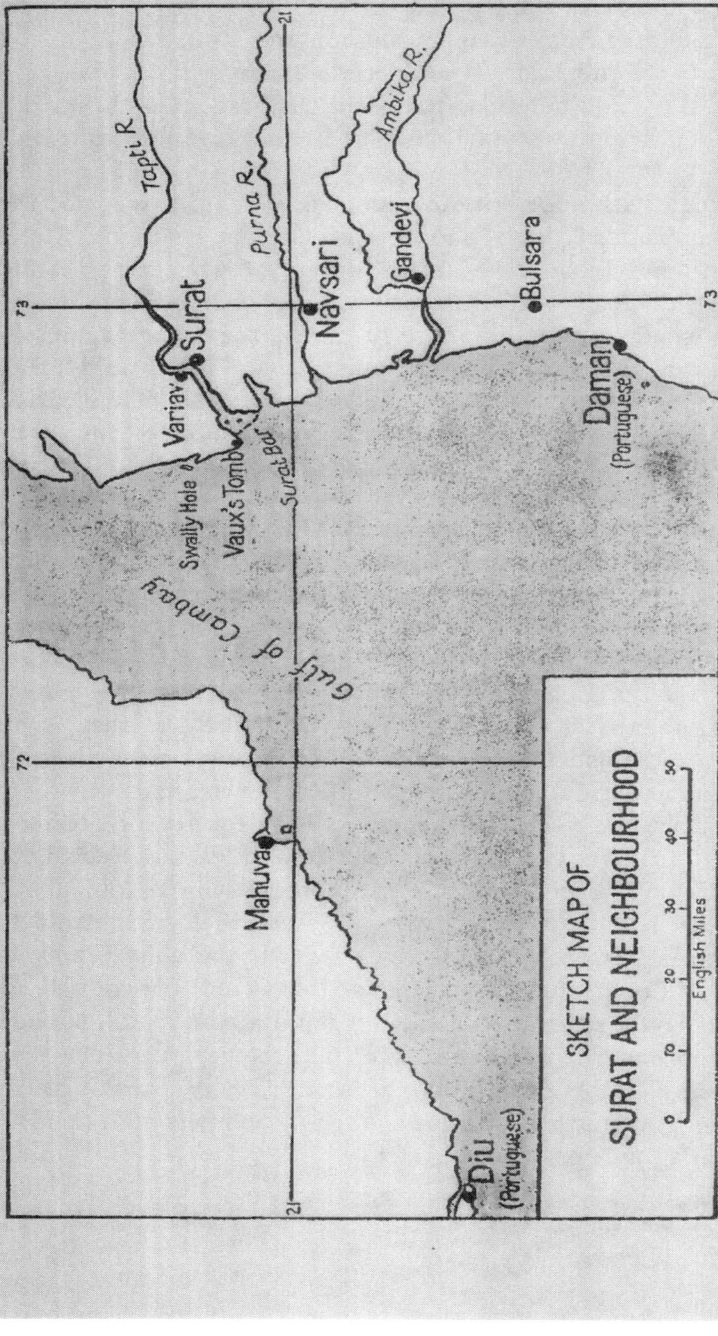
SKETCH MAP OF
SURAT AND NEIGHBOURHOOD
0 10 20 30 40 50
English Miles
Tapti R.
Purna R.
Ambika R.
Surat
Variav
Navsari
Gandevi
Bulsara
Daman
(Portuguese)
Swally Hole
Vaux's Tomb
Surat Bar
Gulf of Cambay
Mahuva
Diu
(Portuguese)
21
72
73

Sic exit Coryatus, and Terry, usually a vile versifier, composed an epitaph for him of which some lines are worth quoting:

> Here lies the Wanderer of his age,
> Who living did rejoice,
> Not out of need, but choice,
> To make his life a Pilgrimage.
> * * * * *
> Many the places which he eyed;
> And though he should have been
> In all parts yet unseen,
> His eye had not been satisfied.
>
> To fill it when he found no room,
> By the choice things he saw
> In Europe and vast Asia
> Fell blinded in this narrow Tomb.[1]

Among other queer visitors whom Terry encountered at Surat were a young English nobleman and two Spanish renegades from Goa.[2] The Englishman, who had been taken up out of pity by Sir Thomas Roe, distinguished himself by beating a servant, and afterwards firing a pistol at him, for which he was sent home. The Spaniards seem to have stepped straight out of the pages of *Don Quixote*. One of them, who dubbed himself the Knight of the Golden Rapier, had been forced to flee from Goa on account of his prowess in duelling. 'He further added that he was now resolved not to live any longer among Christians, but that he desired to live among the English; but when we replied that we were Christians, he cried, *Jesu Maria*, as wondering at it, and further told us that he had never heard so before'. He was entertained at the factory and proved himself a valiant trencherman, but being made to sit among the servants, a position unbecoming to an hidalgo of Spain, he desired the factors to make a little purse for him, 'on which he would live as long as he could, and then creep into some desart place and there repent and die'. However, he seems to have changed his mind, for Terry found him, six months later, alive and well, at the Mughal Court. The second gentleman was, when Terry met him, 'a walking skeleton, most miserably clothed, the

[1] Terry, *Voyage* (1777), p. 73. [2] *Ibid.*, p. 158 ff.

poorest and leanest creature that ever mine eyes beheld.' He had forsaken his religion and turned Muhammadan, but the factors generously clad him and gave him a passage to Plymouth. At sea, however, somewhat illogically 'he would often curse and ban and cry out *O mal ventura!* and that of all the miseries which he had endured, this was the greatest, that he, an Hidalgo, a gentleman of Spain, should live to become a servant and which was worse, to serve an Heretick'.

In 1621 Thomas Kerridge returned to England for a well-earned rest, and Thomas Rastell succeeded him. The English factory at Surat was still eager to develop the trade with Persia which had made such a profitable beginning, and their agent Monnox persuaded their fleet to assist the Persians in the great attack upon Ormuz which has already been described. This remarkable feat of arms, though destined to lead to far-reaching results, brought, however, at the time very little profit to the Company. The lion's share of the spoil went to the Persians, who recouped their allies very tardily, and most of the rest found its way in the shape of loot into the pockets of the officers who took part in the operations; further more James and Buckingham demanded £10,000 apiece for the trouble of answering awkward questions on the part of the Spanish ambassador![1] Altogether it was not a very lucrative undertaking. Rastell now embarked upon another rather desperate venture. The English merchants had long been exasperated by their failure to get any redress for a long list of grievances, the Mughal officials retorting to their complaints with countercharges of piracy on the part of English vessels, for which the Company disclaimed responsibility. Rastell thereupon determined to withdraw, quietly and gradually, all the merchants at outlying factories to Surat, and in the meantime to equip a squadron to go to Aden and seize the Mughal shipping in the Red Sea. These vessels were to be detained as hostages until all claims were settled. The first part of the plot was carried out successfully enough, and when in October 1623 Captain Hall returned from his raid escorting eight captured junks, Rastell slipped on board a vessel lying in the Tapti, whence he could treat in safety.

[1] See p. 77, note 1.

The Surat merchants were very upset at the seizure of their merchandise, and the Nawab of Surat, after trying in vain to enlist the Dutch factors on his side, agreed to parley. Rastell thereupon presented a statement of *The wrongs, oppressions, losses and hindrances sustained by the English Nation living under the protection and tyrannous government of Sultan Khurram and his officers, justly and exactly claimed and particularized.*[1] These claims came to just under £100,000, and the chief items were 900,000 *mahmudis* (£45,000) for 'the despoiled cafila robbed and surprized by the Deccani army, which they do lawfully challenge at the hands of the Great Moghal', on the somewhat far-fetched ground that Malik Ambar (the general of the Nizam Shahi government of Ahmednagar) had since become a subject of Jahangir; and 600,000 *mahmudis* for certain cases of coral which they had imported but had not been allowed to sell. In addition to this, other important concessions were demanded, including the right of free trade at Surat, Cambay, Gogo, Sind, and Bengal; freedom from oppression and extortion on the part of local officials; the lease from Khwaja Hassan Ali of his house at Surat for a factory, 'with garden, stable, and other conveniences'; liberty to build frigates, bear arms, try their own servants in disputes with natives; and to compound customs dues for 40,000 *mahmudis* per annum. Failing redress, Rastell threatened to break up the Surat factory and to sail away to Persia with his prizes. At this the Nawab, apparently cowed, gave in. Unfortunately the English had forgotten one thing which the native authorities had not. Their position depended entirely upon the fleet; once that had sailed beyond recall, they were powerless. And so, one morning in February 1624, the Nawab, acting on orders from Agra, arrested the President and the whole of the Surat factory. They were kept in close confinement.

'All of us imprizoned and in irons', writes Rastell to the Company, 'to be the shameful subjects of daily threats, revilings, scorns and disdainful derisions of whole rabbles of people, whose revengeful eyes never glutted themselves to

[1] *English Factories*, 1622–3, p. 283.

behold the spectacle of our miseries; our warehouses, chambers, and private men's chests in the meantime ransacked, and all that was gold and silver possessed, made sale and disposed of at their pleasures towards satisfaction of the merchants' pretences, whom nothing contenting but money, were so far the aggravators of our sufferings, as that torture itself was the next we hourly expected, to exact the confession of treasure. To pack and stifle us together into close and airless, unwholesome corners, and to abridge us of natural sustenance, were their common practises and refuge whensoever upon the least occasion of standing out with them they had intent to constrain our yielding, which by this course of famishment was against the power of nature in us to contend in.'[1]

Finally, 'business at a dangerous stand through the kingdom and the apparent loss of a monsoon in hazard, if some speedy recourse of remedy were not resolved on to rejoint again our proceedings', a compromise was come to. The junks were restored and the owners agreed to receive recompense in kind for their wrongs, and in the following September a new agreement between the factors and the authorities was signed which included most of the terms of the former one, excepting, however, the right to bear arms, or try Muhammadans. But the treaty was a distinct step forward, embodying as it did several important concessions. It was no small thing for the factors to have obtained a written promise that they should be no longer subject to petty extortions from local officials; that their goods should be free from toll; that they should have their factory on a yearly lease; and that they should be free to trade unhindered throughout the empire.

Of life in Surat in the days of Rastell we have a very interesting account from the pen of Signor Pietro della Valle, an Italian, who, in order to cure a broken heart, took a long tour in the East between 1614 and 1626. At Bagdad he found consolation in a beautiful young Armenian of the name of Maani, but she died near Ormuz, leaving on the traveller's hands a girl named Maria Tinatin. The pair continued their wanderings accompanied by the Signora's embalmed body, which Della Valle had determined to bury in the *Ara Coeli*

[1] *English Factories*, 1624–9, p. 56.

beside the bones of his ancestors. And this he did. He himself sleeps by her side, having first espoused Maria Tinatin, who lived to bear him fourteen sons. He embarked from Bandar Abbas in January 1623 on the *Whale*, Captain Woodcock, having been delayed by the English operations off Ormuz, and arrived at Surat in the following month. The sailors, we are told, objected to carrying a corpse (though the coffin was concealed in a bale of cotton), and mention is made more than once in the contemporary files of disposing of the 'Roman gentleman's goods' as expeditiously as possible.

On their arrival at Surat,

'the President of the English Merchants, (who used to reside at Surat and is superintendent of all their trade in East India and Persia, with other places depending on the same, now one Mr. Thomas Rastell,) perceiving our ships near and being at that time at the sea-shore near the landing-place, came in our boat to the ships, together with one of their Ministers (so they call those who exercise the office of priests) and two other Merchants; and after a collation and a supper, lodged with us all night. He spoke Italian very well and made me many civil offers and compliments, shewing himself in all things a person sufficiently accomplished and of generous deportment, according as his gentle and graceful aspect bespoke him.' [1]

Della Valle did not think the English factory, which was an exclusively bachelor establishment, quite a proper place for his young charge, who went to lodge with an Italian lady; this apparently offended the President, who was 'Not At Home' when Della Valle called. However, the quarrel was presently made up, and the traveller speaks in cordial terms of the hospitality he received. Every one, he tells us, lived 'much after a genteel way', servants costing three rupees a month,[2] and slaves being cheap. Rastell and the Dutch President used to 'have carried before their coach or horse when they ride a very high bannerol or streamer, by a man on foot, and likewise a saddled horse led by hand before them'.[3] They lived in 'sufficient splendour and after the manner of the greatest persons of the country'.

[1] *Travels*, ed. E. Grey (Hakluyt Society), i. 19.
[2] The rupee was then at 2*s*. 9*d*.
[3] *Op. cit.*, p. 41.

Rastell went home in March 1625, and was succeeded by the veteran Kerridge, who was equally popular with factors and Indians.[1] Kerridge's second term of office was distinguished by the fierce fighting in the Persian Gulf between the Anglo-Dutch fleet and the Portuguese under Botelho, Kerridge himself being present at the most important action. This, as we have already noticed, led to a visit on the part of the English ships to the harbour of Bombay, and a proposal to seize and fortify it was actually made by the Company. Kerridge, however, opposed the idea.

'We have seriously considered your advice concerning fortification and are greatly perplexed we cannot give you hope of any to be effected in these parts. Bombay, whereof you have been informed, is no ill air, but a pleasant, fruitful soil, and excellent harbour as experience of our own people doth testify. But the difficulties for you alone to fortify there make it many ways inconvenient, if not impossible to be accomplished, seeing the Portugal, whose country it is, will with their utmost force prevent its commence and be perpetual disturbers of the prosecution.' [2]

Kerridge returned to England in 1628, and was succeeded by Richard Wylde. Sir Thomas Herbert visited the factory during his period of office.[3] He landed at Swally, where he found the Banyans had pitched their 'booths, and tents and huts of straw in great numbers, resembling a country-fair or market'; here calico, China satin, escritoires of mother-of-pearl, jewels, rice, sugar, plantains, and arrack were for sale. Peons, 'olive-coloured Indian foot-boys who can very prettily prattle English', could be hired 'for four pice a day (2 pence of our money) either to interpret, run, go arrands or the like'. Surat was in his opinion an ugly town.

'The *Medon* (*maidan*) is of no great beauty, nor do the shops give more than common splendor: the *Bannyan* desiring rather to be rich indeed, than so accounted. The houses are indifferent beautiful; some (as to the outside) are of

[1] An Indian merchant writes that 'he hath deserved these people's loves', by his 'good carriage and commendable demeanor' (*English Factories*, 1624–9, p. 325).

[2] *Ibid.*, p. 159.

[3] *Travels* (1665 ed.), pp. 43–5.

carved wood, others of bricks dryed in the sun; the *English* and *Dutch* houses at the north end excel the other for space and furniture. . . . The *English* garden without the town has pretty walks and adorned with a variety of sweet flowers.'

Mr. Wylde, says Herbert, was an 'ingenious and civil merchant'. But from other sources we learn that he was a bad President. Discipline was poor; prayers were neglected, Sundays were spent in feasting, drinking, and gambling, and 'the beastly sin of whoredom and most polluted filthy talk, the daily common discourse at meals', were rife. Bribes were freely taken by the authorities to ship private goods free of charge on the Company's vessels; business was left to shroffs and 'banyans', who battened on the factory, and all, from the President downwards, indulged in private trade.[1] Under the circumstances, the Company decided to recall him, but Wylde anticipated their order by voluntary resignation, and Rastell returned in 1630.

Rastell came out with special orders to make a clean sweep of private trade and of all concerned in it. He set about his task with the vigour which had characterized his last term of office, but shortly afterwards was carried away in a tragic manner. In 1630 the monsoon failed; in the following year, the rain fell in torrents, sweeping away fields and crops. The consequence was one of those awful famines which periodically devastated India.

'When we came to the city of Surat', writes a Dutch factor,[2] 'we hardly could see any living persons, where heretofore were thousands; and there is so great a stench of dead persons that the sound people that came into the town were with the smell infected, and at the corners of the street the dead lay twenty together, one upon another, nobody burying them. The mortality in this town is and

[1] *English Factories*, 1630–3, p. 16. Perhaps to be taken *cum grano*, as the author, Boothby, hated Wylde. It is curious to note that the Council encouraged officials to write privately to them about their superiors, and censured Wylde for opening Boothby's letter.

[2] *Ibid.*, p. 181. A vivid account of the famine, called by the natives the *Satāsio Kāl*, or famine of '87 (Samvat 1687), is to be found in *Peter Mundy's Travels*, ed. Temple, vol. ii (Hakluyt Society, 1914). Mundy went to Patna in November 1630 and returned in May 1633. In the meantime fourteen out of the twenty-one English factors had perished.

hath been so great that there have died above 30,000 people. The English house and ours is as if one came into the hospital of Batavia. There is dead of the English factors ten or eleven persons, and of ours three. Those that remain alive of the English are very sorrowful for the death of Mr. Rastell their President, who died about twenty days sithence.'

The English factory was terribly crippled by the loss of their factors and by the paralysis of their trade, and was only able to survive at all by the profits reaped on their Persian goods, especially silk. By the end of 1632, it was in debt to the extent of £90,000.

Joseph Hopkinson, who was elected to fill the post of President, pending orders from England, was himself too ill to do anything except to frame some rules for the discipline of the factory. Persons remaining out after the gates were shut were to be 'amerced to pay forty shillings to the poor'.[1] They were also to be fined for swearing, drunkenness, and absence from Divine Service. Three days' imprisonment in irons was the penalty for striking or abusing outsiders.

APPENDIX TO CHAPTER VI

PRESIDENTS OF SURAT 1613–62

Thomas Aldworth, 1613–15.
Thomas Kerridge, 1616–21.[2]
Thomas Rastell, 1621–5.
Thomas Kerridge, 1625–8.
Richard Wylde, 1628–30.
John Skibbow (acting), April–September, 1630.
Thomas Rastell, 1630–1.
Joseph Hopkinson, 1631–3.
William Methwold, 1633–9.
William Fremlin, 1639–44.
Francis Breton, 1644–9.
Thomas Merry, 1649–52.
Jeremy Blackman, 1652–5.
John Spiller, 1656–7.
Henry Revington, 1657–8.
Nathaniel Wyche, 1658–9.
Matthew Andrews, 1659–62.
Sir George Oxinden, 1662.

[1] *Ibid.*, p. 303.
[2] Title of President came into use *c.* 1618. *Agent* was also used.

CHAPTER VII

THE INTERLOPERS, 1633–9

On November 7, 1633, Hopkinson was succeeded by William Methwold. Methwold was in many respects a remarkable man. He was a scholar of distinction; he had contributed a chapter to Purchas's famous work, and spoke Dutch fluently. he had already had a thorough training in the Company's affairs at their Masulipatam factory. Methwold's first care on his arrival was to do his utmost to repair the damage done by the famine, which had come very near to ruining the Surat factory altogether. Obviously the first thing to be done was to put an end to the lingering hostility with the Portuguese, which had long ceased to profit either party. He therefore set to work at once to negotiate a treaty with Goa, overtures for which had been put forward by Kerridge and Rastell and scornfully rejected. Now, however, neither side was in a condition to continue the struggle. The poverty of Goa was only equalled by her pride, and the English were utterly crippled by the famine. Besides, both parties viewed with apprehension the growing power of the Dutch, who helped the English when it suited them, but were dangerous allies. Preliminaries were arranged by the help of Father Tavares and other influential priests, who were as eager now to help the English as their predecessors had been to oppose them. Methwold and his Council then proceeded to Goa, which they reached on January 6, 1635, amid much firing of guns and other courtesies.[1] They had a long interview with the Viceroy, at the end of which they concluded 'not only a cessation, but union of arms, against the common enemies'.[2] The terms were then drawn up in detail and dispatched to Europe. Methwold was at first inclined to suspect that

[1] *English Factories*, 1634–6, p. 88 ff.

[2] They were 'to observe the like peace here in East India, as hath been so happily begun and continued between our illustrious Princes and their subjects respectively in the parts of Europe' (*ibid*., p. 21–2).

'not love towards us but hate to the Hollanders hath in policy humbled them, that, our opposition being taken off by a neutrality, they may the better vanquish them first; whilst we shall have the favour which was promised unto Ulysses from Polyphemus, in being last devoured'. However, the suspicion was an unworthy one, and when Portugal became free from the clutches of Spain in 1640 the peace was made permanent. It proved advantageous to both sides, and from this time onwards, English ships plied up and down the coast and anchored in Portuguese harbours without hindrance. Another scheme of Methwold's was to abandon the Surat factory altogether and to remove the English head-quarters to Ahmedabad, with Gogo and Cambay as ports of call.

Before, however, these ideas could be discussed, a fresh storm broke upon the Company. Without a word to them, Charles I, in direct violation of the Charter, had licenced one Samuel Bonnell, an employé of Sir William Courten (of whom more anon), to fit out an expedition 'to range the seas all the world over', and 'to make prize of all such the treasures, merchandizes, goods and commodities, which to his best abilities he shall be able to take of infidels, or any other prince, potentate or state not in league with us beyond the line equinoctial'.

It is difficult to imagine anything more scandalous than a licence to commit piracy upon unoffending vessels, couched in such terms. The holders promptly took advantage of it. They fitted out two ships, the *Samaritan* and the *Roebuck*, under one William Cobbe, flying the colours of the Royal Navy, and dispatched them for Aden in April 1635. The *Samaritan* was wrecked, but the *Roebuck* held up two junks, the *Mahmudi* of Diu and the *Taufiqui* of Surat, and cruelly tortured the crew of the latter.

'They took the *nakhuda* (master), and bound both his hands and tied match to his fingers, which burnt them unto the bones; and then he confessed where the money lay and so brought aboard all the *reals*. Then the English said, here be the reals; where be the *ibrahims*? [1] Then they burnt

[1] Turkish coin.

the *nakhuda*, the boatswain, the merchants and the carpenters, until they were near dead and confessed all they knew.'[1]

To make matters worse, the *Taufiqui* belonged to Mirza Mahmud, a great Surat merchant and a loyal supporter of the English factory.

One day Methwold heard a report that English pirates had been plundering Indian vessels. He repaired to the Governor's house to contradict what he thought a ridiculous bazaar rumour, and found there 'a sad assembly of dejected merchants, some looking through me with eyes sparkling with indignation, others half dead in the sense of their loss'. Amid a profound silence the Governor questioned him as to the whereabouts of the English vessels, to which Methwold truthfully replied that he only knew of the *Crispiana*, apparently delayed by a breakdown. Thereupon the Governor read out a letter received from the *Taufiqui*, whereupon 'the whole Company (which had all this while bit in their anger) mouthed at once a general invective against me and the whole English nation; which continued some time with such a confusion as I knew not to whom to address myself unto to give a reply until they had run themselves out of breath'.[2] Methwold in vain argued that it might be French or Dutch pirates, but presently the *Taufiqui* herself put into port, and further denials were useless. A guard was set on the factory, and Methwold was locked up at night in a filthy, airless chamber, swarming with vermin, while by day 'they brought upon us the clamorous swarm of the offended multitude of pretenders; and now we sat, the scorn and object of their opprobrious revilings, until they had wearied themselves with the confusion of noise and most insolent language'. Finally, Methwold settled the claims as far as he could with the cash and goods which he had in hand, and a formal reconciliation was effected. In the meantime the pirates were run to earth by John Proud, master of the *Swan*, off the Comoros. Proud arrested Cobbe, but the crew took up an impregnable position on a neighbouring hill, where they had mounted four 'great

[1] Letter to Mirza Mahmud (*English Factories*, 1634–6, p. 199).
[2] Methwold's narrative (*ibid.*, p. 232 ff.).

pieces' commanding the ship. Proud did not dare to attack them, so he came to a compromise, Cobbe handing over the money and jewels, amounting to £9,700, taken from the Surat boat.[1] Shortly after, the *Blessing*, sent by Methwold, arrived on the scene, and Cobbe took to his heels. He landed in England in 1637 with nearly £40,000 worth of booty, and the Company prosecuted him in vain.[2]

Worse, however, was to follow. Courten, encouraged by the ease with which the first body of 'interlopers' had obtained sanction for their nefarious work, now started an expedition to the Indies upon a really large scale. He collected a fleet of six vessels, for which he paid no less than £120,000, and placed it under Captain Weddell, an old servant of the Company. Indeed, the expedition, from one point of view, may be looked upon as a rival concern, organized by discontented or discharged Company's servants, who used the knowledge gained in its service to spite their former masters. 'If fines and undeserved public reproaches, instead of remuneration for honest service, be the East India Company's favours and honours (as now-a-days they are), we pray God keep both you and us from such indulgences', writes Weddell to the Company.[3] The King's excuse for his action was that he was 'credibly informed that the East India Company had neglected to plant and settle trade in those parts, and had made no fortifications to encourage any in future times to adventure thither, contrary to the practice of the Dutch and Portuguese'; and he goes on to state that 'this neglect has resulted in loss of trade to His Majesty's subjects, as evidenced not only by the complaints of some of the adventurers, but especially by the decrease of the royal customs, which is due to the said Company's supine, neglected discovery of trade in divers places in those parts'.[4] The new Association was authorized to trade on the African and Arabian coasts, in the Persian Gulf, along the Malabar, Coromandel and Bengal coasts, and was specially

[1] Report, *ibid.*, p. 265.

[2] It was owned that 'Mr. Porter had nothing to do with the business, his name only being used, and what was done was his Majesty's act (*I. O. Records, Court Book* 17, p. 385).

[3] *Op. cit.*, p. 323.

[4] *Court Minutes*, 1635-9, p. 127 ff.

enjoined to put into Goa and make an arrangement with the Portuguese Government. After that, the fleet was to proceed to the Far East, and open trade with Siam, China, and Japan, and finally, if possible, to return home by the North-West passage. Charles somewhat illogically assured the Company, on the word of a 'Christian King', that the new Association should not compete against them, ignoring the fact that they were doing so in a most ruinous fashion by the mere fact of diverting English capital at a time when it was most sorely needed. The expedition reached the Comoro Islands in August 1636, and Goa (where they were courteously but coldly received) in October. Weddell sent a polite note to Methwold, saying that he 'could not forget to wish well to his old masters' and enclosing the King's commission ordering the President and Council of the East India Company to render them assistance. Methwold wrote a furious reply, accusing Weddell's promoters of being responsible for 'Cobbe's pranks' and containing other 'flashes and peremptory jeering menaces', which Weddell answered in a similar strain. He was particularly nettled at the imputation of piracy, which he considered a slur upon a respectable Association, trading under Royal Warrant. Weddell went on to the small port of Bhatkal on the Malabar coast, where he obtained permission from the local raja to found a factory for trading in pepper. It was an unhealthy spot, and the graves of members of the little band may still be seen in a tiny cemetery on the edge of the sea. It is pleasant to add that a chivalrous action on his part relieves the somewhat sordid story of the quarrel between the rival companies. A small vessel, the *Comfort*, on its way from Bantam to Surat, was attacked by the notorious pirates of Malabar. A desperate struggle followed. The pirates boarded the ship, and the master, Walter Clark, determined to blow it up rather than surrender. This, however, he reports,

'seemed little or nothing to diminish or quell their courage; but we still continued to defend the opposing enemy by murthering and wounding each other, they being so resolute that they would not step aside from the muzzle of our ordnance when we fired upon them, but immediately being fired, heave in whole buckets of water; insomuch that in the conclusion we were forced to betake ourselves unto the gun deck, upon which we had but two pieces of ordnance. They then cutting with axes the deck over our heads, and hearing the hideous noise and cry of such a multitude, we thought how to contrive a way to send them all to their great adorer, Belzebub, which was by firing all our powder at one blast, as many of us as were alive leaping into the sea, yet intercepted some by those devilish hellhounds'.[1]

The survivors were picked up and imprisoned; however, by the help of a renegade, Henry Weygive, a 'fugitive from the Company and turned Moor', they got into touch with Weddell, who generously ransomed them for 2,200 reals of eight (£550). Tavernier, the French traveller, who was breakfasting with President Fremlin at Surat when the rescued captives arrived, says[2] that they were first ransomed by by the Zamorin of Calicut, who 'would not leave them in possession of the savages, because they were in danger of their lives on account of the 1,200 widows whose husbands were left behind on the two occasions that the ship was on fire', and he adds that the compensation given was 2 *piastres*[3] per widow.

Of life in the English factory in the days of Methwold we are fortunate in possessing an entertaining account from the pen of a contemporary traveller, who enjoyed the factors' hospitality in 1638. This was John Albert de Mandelslo, a young German nobleman, who was sent as an attaché with a diplomatic mission to Persia by the Duke of Holstein. His duties performed, he paid a visit to India, and reached Surat on April 25, 1638. His *Travels*, originally published in 1646, were greatly enlarged by the learned Olearius, and republished, after the author's early death, in 1658.[4]

[1] *English Factories*, 1637–41, p. 139. Cf. Mountney's account on p. 85: 'There are twenty sail of frigates, men of war and robbers, that are abroad, and went out with a full resolution not to come in without they brought with them either English, Dutch, or Portugals. They came up with their white colours as friends, and being full of men, presently entered and overpressed such as they met withal.'

[2] See his *Travels* (transl. Ball), i. 179.

[3] Nine shillings.

[4] A French translation, with magnificent engravings, by De Wicquefort, appeared in 1659, and an English translation by Davies in 1662 and 1669. See V. A. Smith, 'The Credit Due to Mandelslo', *J. R. A. S.*, 1915, p. 245. The passage given is in Davies's version, p. 18 ff., 1662 ed. (p. 12, 1669 ed.).

'At the entrance of the House', he tells us, 'I met the President with his Second, that is to say, he who commands under him and in his absence, whose name was Mr. Fremling, who received me with extraordinary kindness, and very civilly answered the compliment I made him, upon the freedom I took to make my advantage thereof. The President, who spoke Dutch very well, told me I was very welcome; that in the country where we then were, all Christians were obliged to assist one another, and that he was the more particularly obliged thereto as to what concerned me, in respect of the affection I would have expressed towards some of his nation at Ispahan. He thereupon brought me to his chamber where there was a collation ready. It consisted of fruits and preserves according to the custom of the country. As soon as we were set, he asked me what my design was, and understanding that I intended to return for Germany within twelve months, he told me I was come too late to get away that year, by reason no more ships would come that way, but that if I would stay with him five or six months, till there were a convenience of passage, he would take it kindly; that during that time he would contribute all he could to my divertisement: that he would find out a means how I might see the most eminent places in the country,—nay, that he would send some of his own nation along with me, who should find me those accomodations I could not otherwise hope for. This obliging discourse soon prevailed with me to accept of these proffers, so that he shewed me all the house that I might make choice of a convenient lodging, which I took near his Second's chamber. In the evening some merchants and others belonging to the President came and brought me from my chamber to supper into a great hall, where was the Minister with about a dozen merchants, who kept me company, but the President and his Second supped not, as being accustomed to that manner of life, out of a fear of overcharging their stomachs, digestion being slowly performed by reason of the great heats, which are as troublesome there in the night time as in the day. After supper the Minister carried me into a great open gallery, where I found the President and his Second taking the coolness of the sea-air. This was the place of our ordinary rendezvous, where we met every night: to wit, the President, his Second, the principal Merchant, the Minister and myself; but the other merchants came not, but when they were invited by the President. At dinner he kept a great table, of about fifteen or sixteen dishes of meat, besides the dessert.

'The respect and deference which the other merchants have for the President was very remarkable, as also the order which was there observed in all things, especially at Divine Service, which was said twice a day, in the morning at six, and at eight at night, and on Sundays thrice. No person in the house but had his particular function, and their certain hours, assigned them as well for work as recreation. Our divertisement was thus ordered. On Fridays, after prayers, there was a particular assembly, at which met with us three other merchants who were of kin to the President, and had left as well as he their wives in England, which day being that of their departure from England, they had appointed it for to make a commemoration thereof, and drink their wives' healths. Some made their advantage of this meeting to get more than they could well carry away, though every man was at liberty to drink what he pleased, and to mix the Sack as he thought fit, or to drink *Palepuntz*,[1] which is a kind of drink consisting of *aqua vitae*, rose-water, juice of citrons and sugar.

'At our ordinary meetings every day, we took only *Thé*, which is commonly used all over the Indies, not only among those of the country, but also among the Dutch and English, who take it as a drug that cleanses the stomach, and digests the superfluous humours by a temperate heat particular thereto. The Persians instead of *Thé* drink their *Kahwa*, which cools and abates the natural heat which *Thé* preserves.'[2]

The English have a fair garden without the city, whither we constantly went on Sundays after Sermon, and sometimes also on other days of the week, where our exercise was shooting at Butts, at which I made a shift to get a hundred Mamoudis (or five pound sterling) every week. After these divertisements, we had a collation of fruit and preserves, and bathed ourselves in a tank or cistern which had five foot water. Some Dutch gentlewomen served and entertained us with much civility. What troubled me most was that my little acquaintance with the English tongue made me incapable of conversation, unless it were with the President, who spoke Dutch.'

[1] i.e. *five* (*pañcha*) ingredients, as given below, water being added.

[2] Tea did not reach England till 1660; on September 25 Pepys 'did send for a cup of tea (a china drinke)'. A duty of 8*d.* a gallon was imposed on it. In 1664 two pounds were sent to Charles II at the cost of £4 5*s.* 0*d.* Two years later 22¾ lb. were shipped at 50*s.* the pound. In 1690, 41,000 lb., were shipped. This was after the Company had started the China trade (Anderson, *English in Western India*, pp. 36-8). Coffee was earlier; the first coffee-house in London was opened in 1652. One was started by a Jew at Oxford in 1650 (*Chambers's Cyclop.*).

Mandelslo afterwards travelled up to Ahmedabad with a *cafila* or caravan laden with 'quicksilver, roenas (which is a root that dyes red), spices, and a considerable sum of money'. They had a strong escort to keep off the Rajputs, 'a sort of highwaymen or *tories*'. Mandelslo stayed at the English factory, and relates, on the authority of the English and Dutch factors, a tyrannical action committed by the Muhammadan Governor.[1] He gave a grand dinner to his European guests, and afterwards cruelly beheaded a whole troupe of sulky nautch-girls, who refused to dance before them. 'Assure yourselves, gentlemen', he explained, 'that if I did not take this course, I should not long be Governor of Ahmedabad!'

Methwold now felt that he had done his duty. He had been greatly harassed by his long contest against the interlopers without and calumniators within the factory walls: 'I know no trouble or misery (sickness only excepted)', he writes to his employers, 'which I have not met withal in this my short employment in India'.[2] He therefore determined to sail on the *Mary*, homeward bound, on January 5, 1639. Before he sailed, he entertained the factors at a sumptuous banquet, enlivened by music and dancing girls, in the course of which he thanked his audience in affecting terms for their loyalty to himself and the Company. He then handed the letters patent to his successor, William Fremlin.[3] With Methwold sailed Mandelslo, who had returned, after an extensive tour inland, to the English factory, where he was voted 'the civillest, modestest and fairest behaved that we have ever known of his age and education'.[4] He was so popular that he was given a free passage. On his way home, Methwold touched at Goa, and also at Cannanore, to settle with Weddell his debts for the ransom of the crew of the *Comfort*. Weddell himself, after an adventurous voyage to Macao and Canton, returned in the following year on the *Dragon*, which was lost at sea with all hands.

[1] Mandelslo was not, as is usually stated, an eye-witness (V. A. Smith, *op. cit.*, p. 252).
[2] *English Factories*, 1637–41, p. 16.
[3] *Op. cit.*, p. 146.
[4] *English Factories*, 1637–41, p. 118.

CHAPTER VIII

THE END OF THE INTERLOPERS AND THE DUTCH WAR, 1639–54

PRESIDENT FREMLIN's term of office was not marked by any events of great importance. The benefits of Methwold's treaty with Goa soon began to be felt, and the English began to build a large number of coasting vessels in local shipyards, which proved much cheaper than ships built in England. They drove a lucrative trade with the Portuguese ports along the shores of western India. They were, it is true, still troubled by the depredations of the Malabar pirates, but here again the 'frigates', a type of vessel in which the Goanese authorities apparently specialized, proved a very useful protection. Thus, in 1640 we hear of the *Hope* being waylaid by eight 'prowes'[1]; but a Portuguese patrol came up in time to rescue the ship, though the marauders got away with prisoners and booty. The former were, as in the case of the *Comfort*, generously ransomed by Courten's factory at Karwar.[2] The *Swan*, from Bantam to Surat with a valuable cargo, was beset by a fleet of sixteen of these 'thievish villains', but the master courageously put his ship straight at them, 'and so daunted them that they disbanded'.[3]

In 1640, the Company decided to extend their trade in the Persian Gulf to Basra. William Thurston and Edward Pearce were dispatched to that port, where they were courteously received by Ali Basha, 'the rebellious Bashaw of the Turk', and made an agreement to open a factory there. The chief exports, they noted, were pearls, specie, dates, and Arab ponies; the imports most in demand were lead, tin, quicksilver, indigo, sugar, coffee, pepper, and other 'poyzed goods', and cloth, though English broadcloths were 'too high priced for these griping Arabs, who are open-mouthed in

[1] The 'prow' (variously spelt) was properly a Malay galley propelled by oars, but the word was often used to denote any small craft (Yule and Burnell, *s.v.*).

[2] *English Factories*, 1637–41, pp. 243, 289.

[3] *Ibid.*, p. 310.

promising but close-fisted, if it come to performance, more than what of necessity they must'. Merchants came from Diarbekir, Mosul, and Aleppo, and a few Janissaries from Bagdad, to trade at Basra.[1]

The factory at Surat was in an unsatisfactory condition, in spite of the efforts of Methwold and Fremlin. The Civil War was now practically inevitable, and trade in England was dislocated. The Fourth Joint Stock, started in 1642, with a capital of £105,000, proved a failure, and the Company had to endure several losses in ships and money. The *Discovery* was lost with all hands in 1644, taking with her a cargo worth £30,000. The *John* was shortly afterwards carried off by its captain under circumstances which will be hereafter described. Added to all this, Charles I, not content with the harm which he had already done, robbed the Company of £63,000. The way in which this happened was as follows. In 1640, Charles was at his wits' end for money to carry out his ill-fated Scotch campaign. His credit was low, the merchants were on the side of his enemies, and nothing was to be had. He then bethought him of a brilliant idea. The Company had on hand a stock of 600,000 pounds of pepper, unsold. Lord Cottington, on behalf of the King, offered to buy it at the current rate of two shillings and a penny per pound. The Company was reluctant to sell. Their sympathies were with the Parliament; they had a long list of grievances against the Court, which remained unredressed. But while they hated the King, they feared him, and he could do them infinite harm by refusing to negotiate on their behalf with the Dutch or Portuguese. So the pepper was handed over, on the word of a 'Christian King' that the bill, amounting to £63,283, would be settled as soon as possible; meanwhile Charles sold the stock for £50,626 cash. Needless to say, the Company never saw a penny of their money again, and a rich cargo, representing the major part of a season's trade, had to be written off the books of the Third Joint Stock, and added to its other heavy losses.

Meanwhile the Company's rivals, Courten's Association,

[1] *English Factories*, 1637–41, pp. 249–51, and 1642–5, p. 58.

TOMB OF FRANCIS BRETON

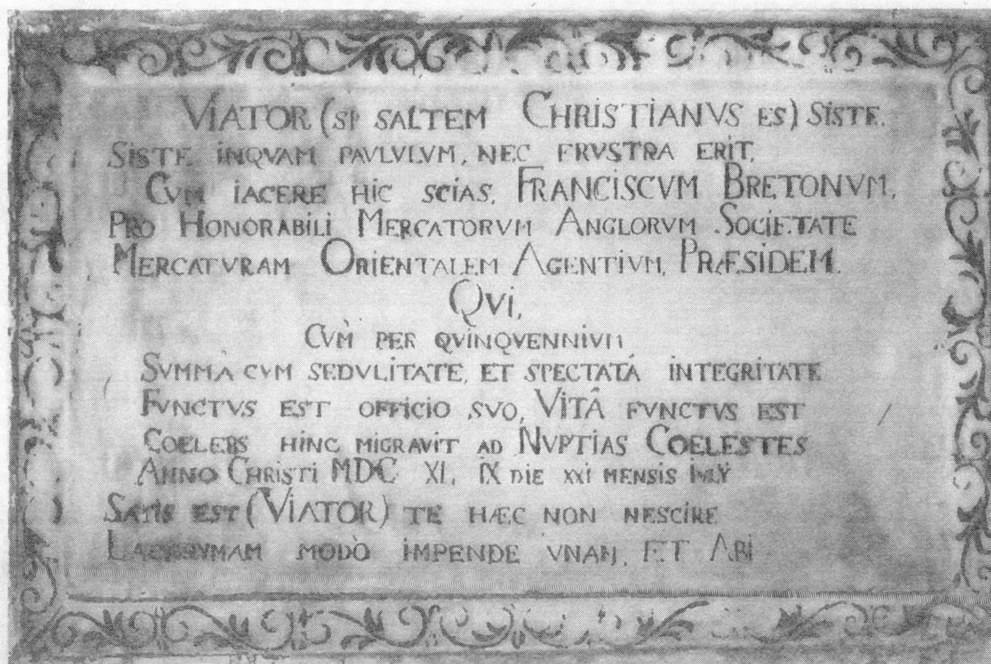

INSCRIPTION IN THE TOMB OF FRANCIS BRETON

were faring no better. Their factory at Bhatkal,[1] after all the money spent on it, had to be removed to Karwar, as the factors found 'Lenten entertainment; for the King, understanding the Viceroy's dislike, refused to admit them entrance'.[2] In 1639, a mission was sent to Muhammad Adil Shah at Bijapur with presents consisting of a set of knives, spoons, and cups mounted in agate, a pearl richly set, a 'gurgalet', and a 'spitting pot', of the total value of 2,500 pagodas, and in return demanded a *farman* for trade; but it was a bad year for pepper, and little came of it. Between 1639 and 1644 they lost the *William*, the *Talbot*, and the pinnace *Thomasine*, and to crown everything, in that year Weddell himself, the life and soul of the venture, was drowned, and his two vessels, the *Dragon* and the *Katherine*, went down with all hands. The Association now sank into bankruptcy. In a desperate attempt to stave off the inevitable, they started coining debased reals and pagodas, some of which they palmed off on the Surat factors, to the indignation of the latter.[3] In 1646, they issued a piteous appeal to the Company to take over the Karwar factory, which the Company, not unnaturally, refused to do. Shortly after, the native governor seized it to recover the rent, which had been owing for four years, and this was the end of an ill-fated venture. Courten, a ruined man, fled to the Continent, and died there.[4]

Fremlin returned home in 1644, and was succeeded by Francis Breton. He had a disastrous voyage; being caught in the storm which proved fatal to the *Discovery* and to Weddell's fleet. His own ship, the *Dolphin*, had to put back to Surat. He managed to reach England safely in the following year, but died soon after his arrival. In 1644, two remarkable events occurred. The first was the defection of the *John*, outward bound, to which reference has already been made.

[1] Bhatkal, now a small town in the North Kanara district, Bombay, was an important place from the fourteenth to the sixteenth century. The spelling of the name by old writers varies much (*I. G.*, 1908, *s.v.*).

[2] *English Factories*, 1637–41, p. 115.

[3] *Ibid.*, 1646–50, p. 38.

[4] In 1647 the House of Lords gave Courten three years in which to withdraw. This alarmed the Company; quite unnecessarily, for the Association was already extinct (*Court Minutes*, 1644–9, p. xii, introd.).

The master of the *John*, Captain Mucknell, was an amusing character. He hated the Puritans, and was given to drink, under the influence of which he gave vent to his opinions in a dangerous manner. He had already been fined four pounds for speaking of them as 'Roundheaded devils'.[1] On board the ship were Edward Knipe, a leading merchant, and Henry Gary, a mischievous fellow who plays subsequently a leading part in the Company's affairs. With his companions he started to quarrel very soon: he openly spoke of the factors as 'Jack Straw and Wat Tyler', and refused to endure their 'chubbings'. The crisis came when Knipe wanted to let the best cabin to the Portuguese governor of Mozambique and his numerous half-caste family. 'He incensed the seamen against Mr. Knipe for bringing these blacks into the shipping, telling them they would all be poisoned if they stayed long aboard'.[2] Knipe threatened Mucknell with punishment on their arrival at Surat. But Mucknell had other ideas on the subject. 'When he was in his cups', says one of the crew, 'he would say, "I am a Prince at Sea. I am the proudest man on earth: I am a Cockny,[3] that 's my glory!"' And so Mucknell formed the bold plan of marooning his tormentors, and handing over the ship to the King. His plans were made with considerable skill. Pretending to be reconciled with Knipe and Gary, he arranged a picnic on the island of Johanna. In the middle of the feast he slipped aboard, cut the cables and made off. He then assembled the crew and harangued them. Those who disagreed had their ears cropped or were landed at St. Helena. Two of Courten's ships were next waylaid and forced to give up powder and stores. Mucknell then made for Bristol, which was being held by Sir John Pennington for the King. Bristol was then in a state of siege, and shortly afterwards surrendered to Fairfax; but Mucknell managed to slip away.

'Although he came with the ship etc safe into Bristol', we read in the Company's Minutes, 'and there made away with what was found in the ship, yet that was not an end of

[1] *English Factories*, 1642–6, p. 262.
[2] Buckingham's narrative, *ibid.*, p. 263.
[3] Most of the traders were Londoners.

his villany, but others also suffered much by his depredations and robberies in those parts, until some of the Parliament's ships had him in chase and forced him upon the rocks of Scilly, and either there or in Mount's Bay the ship utterly perished. For himself he escaped, to do further mischief until God's hand or the gallows make an end of him.'[1]

The Company's pious wishes apparently were not fulfilled, for we find later that he was hanging about the Canary Isles, preying on Indian shipping, and a gold chain had been offered (apparently without success) for his capture. The party marooned by him on Johanna was taken off by Courten's vessels, and finally reached Surat in the Dutch vessel *Valkenburg*.

The second event of 1644 was the revival of the scheme to plant a colony at Assada, the modern French settlement of Nossi Bé, an island on the north-west of Madagascar. The idea was not a new one; as long ago as 1636 it had been proposed to send out a colony under Prince Rupert, but nothing had been done.[2] The Company was very apprehensive that these colonists would interfere with their Indian trade. However, their fears were groundless. The little band of settlers landed found the struggle against disease and native hostility too much for them. In 1646 the Company's ships, touching at St. Augustine's Bay, found 'divers poor people on shore . . . weary of their employment, . . . and if supplies arrived not suddenly, like to be in a deplorable condition'.[3] In 1649 a fresh body went out under Colonel Hunt in the *Assada Merchant*. But they had no better luck. Hunt and many others died of the 'contagion of the place'; the survivors went over to Madagascar, where the natives murdered most of them. There was now some talk of amalgamating the Assada Merchants with the East India Company,[4] and the members of the United Joint Stock, who wished to start colonies in the East on the Dutch model, were in favour of this course. Major Hartly and fresh settlers afterwards arrived,

[1] Quoted in *Court Minutes*, 1644–9, p. viii, introd.
[2] *Court Minutes*, 1635–9, p. xxiii, introd.
[3] *English Factories*, 1646–50, p. 1.
[4] *Court Minutes*, 1644–9, pp. 369, 374, 387, &c.

but finding conditions impossible, abandoned the 'plantation' and went on to Surat, where most of them found service with the Company. Subsequent reinforcements arrived too late, and the idea was finally abandoned.[1]

In 1649 Breton died, and was buried in a stately tomb, the first of the fine structures raised over the bones of the English Presidents in the graveyard at Surat. The inscription thereon informs us that '*cum per quinquennium summâ cum sedulitate et spectatâ integritate functus est officio suo, . . . coelebs hinc migravit ad coelestes nuptias*'. The factory had now branches at Ahmedabad, Agra, Lucknow, Tatta, Baroda, Broach, Basra, and Gombroon. In 1652 Merry was succeeded by Captain Jeremy Blackman, in whose favour the Company made several important concessions. His pay as President was to be £500 per annum, to commence from his departure from England, with £40 allowance for servants. He was permitted, as a special favour, to take his wife with him. This was a most unusual thing, no wives of English merchants having visited Surat since the escapades of Mrs. Towerson and Mrs. Steele. Mrs. Blackman must have felt strange in the bachelor establishment in which she found herself, though she had, of course, the companionship of the ladies of the Dutch factory. This, however, was destined not to last for very long. In 1652 the long commercial rivalry between the two nations led to the outbreak of war. The factors at Surat made the usual mistake of underrating the enemy. They were confident, they write, that 'our people would show themselves Englishmen here in India as well as our friends at home, where one Englishman thinks himself as good as two Dutchmen, and by God's blessing have proved themselves so'[2]. They were to find, however, that the well-equipped Hollanders were opponents very different from the gallant but ill-equipped Portuguese. Most of the fighting was in the Persian Gulf, a new field of trade which both sides were endeavouring to exploit. The *Lannerett* and the *Roebuck* ran into the Dutch fleet. The *Roebuck's* mast was brought down; a tangle of

[1] *Court Minutes*, 1650–4, pp. ix–xi, introd., *et passim*.
[2] *English Factories*, 1651–4, p. 146.

sails and cordage fell among the batteries and caught fire; the crews took to their boats and surrendered. The *Lannerett* had her rudder smashed, and drifted ignominiously into the Dutch admiral and was captured. The Dutch towed her in triumph to Gombroon with the British ensign trailing astern. The victors were much elated, and it was 'much admired by the country-people that a Dutchman should make prize of an Englishman'. The loss of prestige, so carefully built up since the time of Roe by able diplomacy and successive victories over the Portuguese, was serious. President Blackman warned the Company that the impression of English inferiority must be dispelled, or 'you must bid adieu to your East India trade'. He pointed out that what was chiefly needed was a permanent port of their own, to serve as a depôt and naval base for the English, where they would not be at the mercy of a native potentate, thus confirming an idea which was steadily gaining ground among the younger members of the Company. He suggested that Portugal might be willing to give up Bombay, Bassein or Mozambique.[1] The idea was put before Cromwell, but nothing came of it.[2] Blackman also complains of the insubordination caused by the presence of a number of unattached Englishmen not under the control of the Company—interlopers and independent traders, and members of Courten's Association and of the Assada plantation. 'There are those with us that call themselves Freemen, that are very pernicious in their actions to us, being companions to all such of our people as they find discontented, and not only inveigle them from your service, but convey them to the Dutch or Moors as they find them most inclined', he writes.[3]

Clearly something was badly wrong with the discipline aboard the Company's ships, and the sailors showed little of the fine spirit which had been displayed under Best and Downton. The *Supply* and *Blessing* were the next victims, the crew of the former throwing down their arms after a fight lasting seven hours.[4] Early next year a fresh humiliation

[1] *English Factories*, 1651–4, p. 170.
[2] *Court Minutes*, 1650–4, p. 374.
[3] *English Factories*, 1651–4, p. 252. *Op. cit.*, p. 191.

was suffered. An English squadron consisting of the *Endeavour*, the *Welcome*, the *Falcon*, and the *Dove*, from Gombroon to Surat with a cargo of silk, wine and specie, was waylaid off Laribandar by a Dutch fleet of three ships. These were vessels built specially for the purpose, small and low, and heavily gunned.[1] The English, deceived by their appearance, advanced eagerly to the action, hoping to secure an easy victory, and the Hollanders, closing their port-holes, carefully concealed the weight of their batteries till the last moment. The *Falcon* fouled the Dutch admiral and after a hand-to-hand fight lasting for an hour, cut herself loose. A lucky shot (fired, if we can believe his account, by the traveller Tavernier) started a blaze. The majority of the crew, including the notorious Gary, then deserted the ship, and most of them were picked up by the *Welcome*. The panic was needless, for the boatswain and some men who remained aboard, mostly wounded, put out the fire, although they had to surrender next day to superior numbers. Meanwhile, the *Endeavour*, after putting up a fairly good fight against two ships, was holed between wind and water and ran up the white flag. The Dutch put a prize crew on board, and then finding the English sailors in the hold looting the Shiraz wine, joined them in this congenial occupation. Meanwhile the vessel filled and suddenly sank, taking the drunken wretches with it. The *Dove* and *Welcome* now sheered off in the most disgraceful manner, though they might have easily turned the scale by a resolute attack. The Dutch then towed the *Falcon* in triumph to Surat, to the intense humiliation of the factors. As a matter of fact they had little to boast about. 'Never was fight worse mismanaged on both sides', Tavernier told Blackman. 'The Dutch were most of them drunk and knew not what they did. The English were little better, if not worse. They would never else have lost such an opportunity.' Fortunately, however, news now reached the factors of the great actions off the Texel. 'In the end of May last', they write, 'there was a great engagement between the two fleets, wherein, after a very hot dispute, with the loss

[1] See Tavernier's account of the battle, trans. Ball, i. 312 ff.

of twenty-five of their ships, which were burnt, sunk, and taken, and 1,300 prisoners taken, they were forced to fly.' This was followed by another fleet action in which 'upward of thirty ships were all burnt and Admiral Van Trompe slain'.[1] This great blow led to the Peace of Westminster, by which, after prolonged discussion of claims and counter-claims, the Company received a net sum of £85,000 in compensation for various injuries and damages.[2] Unfortunately, the Government borrowed £50,000 of this and there is no record of its repayment. In all probability the matter drifted on until the Restoration, when it was hopeless to expect further redress. The balance of £35,000 was mostly expended in settling various outstanding claims, and very little seems to have actually reached the pockets of the shareholders.[3]

[1] *English Factories*, 1651–4, pp. 197–8.
[2] *Court Minutes*, 1650–4, p. xxi, introd.
[3] *Ibid.*, 1655–9, pp. i-viii, introd.

CHAPTER IX

LIFE IN THE ENGLISH FACTORY IN THE SEVENTEENTH CENTURY

THE Treaty of Westminster really marks the end of a chapter in the history of the Company. President Blackman proceeded to England in the following year, and in 1657 the Company's charter was renewed by the Commonwealth Government. One of the clauses in the new agreement gave them the right to 'fortify and plant in any of their settlements, and to transport thither colonists'. This is the beginning of a new phase, which had been foreseen by many experienced Indian administrators. Surat was insufficient and inadequate for many reasons. The English were at the mercy of the Mughal Governor, who could, and frequently did, exercise his authority by imprisoning them whenever a difference occurred, besides perpetually hampering them by the imposition of extortionate customs dues. But the weakness of their position at Surat was finally demonstrated by the raids of the Marathas under Sivaji, which though temporarily beaten off with success, showed that the town was radically unsafe as a base. Hence, when Charles II obtained Bombay from Portugal, the Company had the opportunity of acquiring a port of their own, where they might imitate the Dutch in founding a permanent and independent seat of trade. We must deal in another place with the transition from Surat to Bombay under the administration of Sir George Oxinden and President Aungier. Meanwhile, we shall attempt to trace in outline something of the life in the great English factory at Surat before its glories were eclipsed by the rise of its later rival, the present capital of Western India. The travellers to whom we have already referred, Della Valle, Herbert, and Mandelslo, have given us a lively picture of factory life as they found and enjoyed it; but their accounts are of little value compared with the detailed descriptions to be found in the works of two later visitors, Fryer and

Ovington,[1] who, though they actually wrote about a quarter of a century later than the period with which we have dealt in the preceding pages, nevertheless describe a state of things which remained substantially unaltered from the days of Kerridge and Methwold until the head-quarters of the Company in Western India was finally transferred to Bombay. Dr. John Fryer came out to Surat as 'chirurgeon' to the factory in 1673; Ovington, a chaplain about whom not very much is known outside his entertaining narrative, sailed on April 11, 1689, the day of the coronation of William III.

The traveller to Surat usually disembarked at the roadstead of Suvali, called by the English Swally Hole or Swally Marine. As we have already seen, this roadstead had been discovered by Sir Henry Middleton, and was used in preference to the mouth of the Tapti, because it left more room for manœuvre in case of attack or sudden squall. Nowadays the once famous anchorage is deserted and lonely, but at that time it presented an animated sight. Vessels of all kinds were busy loading and unloading. Ashore, the stores and godowns of the English, French, and Dutch flew their national flags. The accommodation at Swally was not very elaborate, and no doubt the port was closed down altogether during the monsoon. 'The place admits of little better tenements than booths', writes Fryer.

> 'Before President Andrew's time they always lodged in tents, but since, wooden houses tiled with pantiles [2] have been raised in an inclosure allotted by the Governor. In which compound are included warehouses, stables, and other out-houses, with as good a garden as this sandy soil will allow; in which ours exceeds the other two, being far pleasanter seated.'[3]

On landing, the traveller was beset by a swarm of 'Banyans', the *banyas*, or petty traders who haunt every Eastern port.

> 'As soon as you have set your foot on shore, they crowd in their service, interposing between you and all civil respect,

[1] Fryer, *A New Account of East India and Persia*, 1672–81, edited for the Hakluyt Society by W. Crooke, 1909; Ovington, *A Voyage to Surat in the Year 1689*, by J. Ovington, M.A., Chaplain to His Majesty, London, 1696. The latter has never been reprinted.

[2] Pantiles are tiles with a curved surface.

[3] *New Account*, ed. Crooke, i. 211 ff.

as if you had no other business but to be gulled; so that unless you have some to make your way through them, they will interrupt your going, and never leave till they have drawn out something for their advantage. At this time of shipping they present the Governor of Surat to licence them to keep a mart there, which they make the Europeans pay dearly for; yet such is their policy, that without these neither you nor the natives themselves shall do any business.'[1]

Having avoided these obsequious rogues, the traveller would stay for a meal at one of the factories' huts, after which he would proceed to Surat. The mode of conveyance was either a *hackery*, a two-wheeled chariot drawn by 'swift little oxen', or if the visitor was a person of consequence, a ponderous carriage belonging to the Company, upholstered in silk, and drawn by a pair of the famous milk-white cattle of Gujarat, 'with circling horns as black as coal, each joint tipped with brass, from whence come brass chains across to the headstall, which is all of scarlet, and a scarlet collar to each, of brass bells about their necks, their flapping ears snipped with art, and from their nostrils bridles covered with scarlet'.[2] The road passed by the tombs of various adventurers who had perished soon after landing in India—a sad memorial of the terrible mortality among Englishmen in the East in those days—and through the villages of Damka and Mora, notorious for their 'punch-houses' and other disreputable establishments, where, alas, English sailors might often be seen 'straggling drunk' about the streets.[3] It was not usual for English ladies to come to the East in those days, but if they did, their carriage was made private by *chicks*, or blinds of split bamboo, and provided with an escort which seemed, in their picturesque garb, says Fryer, to be 'such a troop as went to apprehend Our Saviour, after the manner we find them on old landskips, and led by the same phanatik lights we see there painted'. A hot journey of ten miles over indifferent roads through 'brave champion ground' brought the traveller to the banks of the broad and stately Tapti, which lapped the city walls. Here the Company's barge

[1] The reader should compare Ovington's account of the 'Banyans', *op. cit.*, p. 275 ff.
[2] Fryer, i. 213, and cf. i. 295, and iii. 157.
[3] *English Factories*, 1622–3, p. 283.

THE OLD ENGLISH FACTORY

waited to take him across, and if he arrived at sunset, he would be half deafened by the clamour of the drums and trumpets of the *nakkar khana* at the castle, which sounded night and morning when the Muhammadan governor was in residence. Oriental music is not very agreeable to European ears; and Fryer confesses that when he heard it, 'he could think of nothing but the last trump'. Here other coaches awaited the visitor to take him to the factory: on the way he had to pass the custom-house, where he was lucky if his luggage was not thoroughly overhauled by the rapacious officials, and any attractive novelty or trifle appropriated. A drive through the city brought him to the factory. This was one of the best houses in Surat: it was leased for £60 per annum to the Company, but the rent was actually remitted on the understanding that it should be expended in repairs. It was a solid, two-storied building, opening, in Muhammadan fashion, inwards. The outside was plain stone and timber, with good carving 'without representations'. The flat roof and the upper story floors were of solid cement, half a yard thick. Inside was a quadrangle surrounded by cloisters or verandahs. The ground floor was used for the Company's trade; the rooms opening on to it, utilized as stores and godowns, presented a busy scene in the shipping season. 'They live in a continual hurly-burly', says Fryer, 'the banyans presenting themselves from the hour of ten till noon; and then afternoon at four till night, as if it were an exchange in every row; below stairs, the packers and warehouse keepers, together with merchants bringing and receiving musters,[1] make a mere Billingsgate; for if you make not a noise, they hardly think you intent on what you are doing.' 'For the buying and more advantageous disposing of the Company's goods', Ovington adds, 'there are brokers appointed, skilled in the rates and value of all the commodities in India.'[2] These were given 2 to 3 per cent. for their care and trouble; in reality, however, they made much more—how much, it was not safe to inquire, as the factors, being ignorant of the vernacular, were constantly being

[1] Samples (Crooke).

[2] *Op. cit.*, p. 401. Cf. Fryer, i. 217–18.

victimized. To remedy this, the Company offered a reward for proficiency in native languages, and kept a *pundit* to instruct the young writers, but without much success. Only a few exceptional men, like Kerridge, Methwold, and Oxinden ever acquired proficiency as 'linguists' or interpreters.[1]

The upper story was used for living rooms. A handsome suite, with 'noble rooms for counsel and entertainment, pleasant tanks, yards, and an *Hummum* to wash in', was provided for the President. The factors had a large open dining-hall, and an oratory or chapel, 'decently embellished', says Ovington, 'so as to render it both neat and solemn, without the figure of any living creature in it, for avoiding all occasion of offence to the *Moors*, who are well pleased with the innocence of our worship'.[2]

The office of President was one of great dignity and importance, for the President controlled all the English factories in Western India and Persia, and also Bantam for a considerable time. The President was usually appointed from England, and could look forward to honourable employment at the Company's head-quarters after his return, if he acquitted himself well. He had to sign a bond for £5,000 on good security; he received a salary of £500 per annum.[3] Three to five years was the usual term of office. The President lived in state; he dined in his own apartments, except on festive occasions, and went abroad in a palanquin, preceded by guards, flagmen, and mace-bearers, with an ostrich-feather fan, like the noblemen of the Moghal court. Next in importance came the councillors, senior factors, four or five in number, who received from £300 to £100 per annum, according to seniority of service. Of these, the senior member was the accomptant. He ranked next to the President, and was a person of high rank in the eyes of the Company, as through his hands passed the receipts for the whole of India. He was, in fact, the Company's treasurer in the East. Next to him

[1] As Crooke remarks, this disposes of the old myth that modern Anglo-Indians are less proficient in the vernaculars than their forefathers.

[2] *Op. cit.*, p. 404.

[3] Half of this, however, was 'reserved to be received at home, in case of misdemeanour' (Fryer, *op. cit.*, i, p. 217). The same was done in the case of all the factors.

came the warehouse-keeper, 'who registers all Europe goods vended, and receives all Eastern commodities bought'; and the purser, 'who gives account of all goods exported and imported, pays the seamen their wages, provides waggons and porters, looks after tackling for ships and ships stores'. Lastly came the secretary, 'who models all consultations, writes all letters, and carries them to the President and council to be perused and signed; keeps the Company's seal, which is affixed to all passes and commissions; and records all transactions and sends copies of them to the Company'.

Two other leading personages in the factory were the surgeon and the chaplain. The surgeon received £50 per annum, the Company supplying him with drugs, and with a native assistant.[1] The chaplain was a well-known figure. The first regular chaplain was appointed in February 1657 (8), the former incumbents having come out spasmodically as ship's chaplains,[2] or in attendance on people like Sir Thomas Roe.[3] Some of these did not lead very edifying lives.[4] Hence the Company applied to Oxford and Cambridge for suitable candidates.[5] They were promised 'an allowance of £100 per annum certaine, with accommodation of Dyet, and there is noe question but their other benefits will be very considerable'. Besides this, the chaplain had a carriage to ride in and a *peon* to wait on him.[6] Unfortunately, even these measures had not always the desired effect. There are black sheep in every flock, and in a letter dated November 16, 1700,[7] we find a complaint that

'Your Honour's Chaplaine put on board the *De Grave* and approved by the Bishop of London as hee saith and whom he

[1] Ovington, p. 402.

[2] e.g. Henry Lord, 1616, author of the *Discovery of two forreigne Sects*, a work on Hindu and Parsi religion, and Copeland who came in the *Royal James*, 1618.

[3] Hall. Terry, who succeeded Hall as Roe's chaplain, had come out independently.

[4] Golding, whose adventures have been already described.

[5] Yule, *Hedges' Diary*, vol. ii (Hakluyt Society, 1887), p. cccli.

[6] Ovington, p. 404.

[7] Yule, *Hedges' Diary*, vol. ii, p. ccix. The date is given as 1600, but this is an obvious error, curiously not noted. The incident referred to took place at Hugly, but it is quoted as an example of the morals of the time.

esteems his great friend and patron and very good Lord, runn away herefrom and left the Ship and is entered into the Enemies Camp and there remains. Wee understand hee is a very lewd druncken swearing person drencht in all manner of debaucheries and a most bitter enemy to King William and the present Government, and since he did runn away wee are pleased hee hath taken his quarters with them that he may not influence any your servants with his emoralities or doctrines, one whereof is that he is exempt from Secular Power. . . . Wee pray your Honours some effectuall course may be taken for the preventing these and the like in famous scandalls to our Nation and Religion, and that these parts be not stockt with such persons.'

One of the objects of having chaplains was to counteract the influence of the Portuguese Catholic priests.[1] Some mission work 'for the advancement and spreading of the gospell in India '[2] was contemplated at one time, but besides the conversion (1617) of a 'Mogul Atheist', nothing appears to have been done.[3] The chaplain was kept very busy, for the Company's servants were stout Puritans who combined business with a somewhat ostentatious piety, which had not yet been undermined by the dissoluteness of the Restoration. An anonymous writer (probably Sir Streynsham Master),[4] has left an entertaining account of the 'Manners of the English Factors, etc., their way of civil converse and pious comportment and behaviour', in which he describes the chaplain's duties at great length.[5]

'We have prayers every morning before the doors of the Factory are open, and every night between eight and nine o'clock after the doors are shut: upon Sundays we have twice in the day solemn service and sermons read and preached, and prayers at night. This office is performed by the President, and in case of his absence by the chief of the Council or other next in the Factory if there be no Minister (or *Padre*

[1] Anderson, *English in Western India*, p. 25.
[2] Yule, *Hedges' Diary*, vol. ii, p. cccli.
[3] Anderson, *English in Western India*, p. 25.
[4] Quoted in full in Yule, *Hedges' Diary*, vol. ii, p. cccv ff.
[5] No doubt he paints the condition of the factory in rosy hues. He wishes to show that he and his companions have not been 'shaken' by the 'Customes of the heathen Indians', or 'Subtile insinuations of the Jesuits'. If this picture is true it compares very favourably with Calcutta (*vide* Yule, *op. cit.*, p. cccxviii ff.).

as we call them). If there be a Minister in the Factory, then he performs his duty as in Churches in England, catechizing the youth on Sundays after evening service, and administering the Sacrament the three great Festivals of the year, and sometimes oftener, burying the dead, and in these duties we are continually exercised, keeping strictly to the rules of the Church.'

The chaplain had also the duty of visiting the subordinate factories in regular circuit, a toilsome and even perilous task in these days.[1]

Apart from these dignitaries,

'the mass of the Company's servants may be comprehended in these classes, *viz.* Merchants, factors and writers; some Blewcoat boys also have been entertained under notion of apprentices for seven years, which being expired, if they can get security they are capable of employments. The writers are obliged to serve five years for £10 per annum, giving in bond of £500 for good behaviour, all which time they serve under some of the forementioned offices; after which they commence factors, and rise to preferment and trust according to seniority or favour, and therefore have a £1,000 bond exacted from them, and have their salary augmented to £20 per annum for three years, then entering into new indentures, are made senior factors; and lastly, merchants after three years more; out of whom are chose chiefs of factories, as places fall, and are allowed £40 per annum during their stay in the Company's service, besides Lodgings and victuals at the Company's charges.' [2]

What strikes the reader most forcibly is the lowness of the salaries. Even granted that servants cost two or three rupees a month, and that everything else in India in the seventeenth century was on a similar scale, it is difficult to see what inducement even a 'Blewcoat boy' could find to set off against the perils and discomforts of Indian life in a salary of £10 per annum, rising to £20 in five years. We must remember, however, that, as Ovington tells us, the Banyans,

'once a year, which is their grand Festival season, called the Dually (*Divali*) time, have a custom much like that of our New Years-gifts, of presenting the President and Council, the Minister, Surgeon, and all the Factors and Writers with something valuable, either in jewels or plate, *atlasses* or other

[1] Ovington, p. 404.

[2] Fryer, i. 216.

silks, according to the respect which they owe to every man's station. Whereby the young factors, besides their salaries, diet and lodgings, are supplied likewise with clothes sufficient for service a great part of the year. Which things prevent their necessity of any great annual expense, and happily contribute towards giving them a life of delight and ease.'[1]

Thus, 'they all have given them their diet and lodging gratis by the Company, besides wages', continues Ovington,

'and the advantageous liberty of traffick to all parts, wherein from China to Surat, they commonly make cent per cent; they can sometimes make 50 per cent from thence, if they only carry out silver and bring home gold: and those among them that are persons of credit and esteem, but of small fortunes, may borrow from the Banyans money for China at 25 per cent, and that only to be paid upon the safe arrival of the ship, which if it miscarries in the voyage, they are exempt from all damage. To some parts their gains amount to more, to some they are less, according to the distance of ports, and opportunities of trade.'[2]

Even the chaplain made a good deal of money over and above his somewhat slender salary. 'Besides many private gifts from merchants and Masters of ships', says Ovington, 'who seldom fail of some valuable oblation to him, or rarity of the place they come from; he constantly receives noble large gratuities for officiating at Marriages, Baptisms and Burials'.[3] In the same way, the surgeon received handsome fees for outside practice from rich natives. One of the most entertaining chapters of Fryer's work describes his visit to Junnar, to cure the wife of the Muhammadan governor, a 'plump, russet dame', who, after he had bled her, 'poured upon her extravasated blood a golden shower of pagods'.[4]

Fryer supplies us with some interesting information on the subject of the trade at Surat in his time. The Surat district itself produced vast quantities of *Calicuts*, calico or cotton, so called from the place whence they were originally shipped, though Calicut had long since ceased to export this commodity. Owing, however, to the increase in price and decrease

[1] Ovington, pp. 401–2. [2] *Ibid.*, p. 391.

[3] 'The minister and surgeon seldom fail of the President's bounty at the Christmas season,' and the former also got fees for officiating at the Dutch factory. [4] *Op. cit.*, i. 326.

in quantity which was the natural result of the demand, factors were sent to establish smaller stations or factories in Gujarat and other parts, 'to oversee the weavers, buying up the cotton-yarn to employ them all the rains, when they set on foot their investments, that they may be ready against the season of the ships; or else the chief broker employs Banyans in their stead, who is responsible for their fidelity.' Of the collection of goods, not much, it is to be feared to the profit of the poor *rayat*, we have an account in a letter, which, though belonging actually to a much later date, may be quoted here as typical of the methods generally employed.

'Factors or agents called *gomastas*', says William Bolts in his *Considerations on Indian Affairs*,[1] 'are engaged at monthly rates by the gentleman's *banyan*. These are despatched with a *parwana* from the Governor of Calcutta or the chief of a Subordinate, to the *Zamindar* of the district where the purchases are intended to be made. . . . Upon the *gomasta's* arrival at the *aurang*, or manufacturing town, he fixes upon a habitation, which he calls his *kachary*; to which, by his *peons* and *harkaras*, he summons the brokers, together with the weavers; whom he makes to sign a bond for the delivery of a certain quantity of goods, at a certain time and price, and pays them a part of the money in advance.'

Under this system the Banyan or broker was an important person. 'He is interpreter, head book-keeper, head secretary, head broker, the supplier of cash and cash-keeper', says Bolts. 'He conducts all the trade of his master, to whom, unless pretty well acquainted with the country languages, it is difficult for any of the natives to obtain access.'

Of the articles of commerce arriving by *Cafilas* or caravans from the various factories to the entrepôt at Surat for shipment to England, Fryer gives the following list:

From China, via Bantam, in exchange for broadcloth and dollars: Sugar, tea, porcelain, lacquer ware, quicksilver, *Tuthinag* (zinc and pewter alloy), copper.

From Siam and the Philippines: as above, with Cowrie shells, used as small change.

From Sumatra, in exchange for corn: Gold and ivory.

[1] 1772, quoted by Ramsay Muir, *Making of British India*, pp. 89–92.

From Persia: Drugs and fine Carmanian wool.

From Mocha: Coffee.

The Indian factories sent the following supplies:

From Ahmedabad: Silks and gold-embroidered *atlasses* (a kind of satin).

From Agra: Indigo, *chuperly* (shellac), coarse cloth, Siring chintz (a fine cotton), Broach *Baftas* (woven cloth), and dimity, and other fine calicoes.

From Bombay and Rajapur: *Salloos* (Turkey red cotton).

From Karwar: Dungaree cotton cloth and pepper.

From Calicut: Spice, ambergris, garnets, opium, and saltpetre.

'On these wheels', Fryer concludes, 'moves the traffick of the East, and has succeeded better than any Corporation preceding, or open trade licenced in the time of Oliver Cromwell: though how much more to the benefit of England than a free commerce, may be guessed by their already being overstocked with Europe merchandize, which lowers their price. What then would a glut do, which certainly must follow, but debase them more and enhance these?' Bombay, he adds, was a free port, but the independent traders there were in a poor way. Fryer was evidently no Free Trader, and urged cogent reasons in support of the Company's monopoly.

It is possible, from the accounts which have come down to us, to picture fairly accurately daily life in Surat in the seventeenth century. Rising at dawn, the factor would 'comfort the stomach' with 'burnt wine'. At six he would hurry to the chapel, unless he wished to incur the fine of half a crown for non-attendance. After prayers, the factory gates would be thrown open, and the Banyans and traders would stream in. Till noon, pandemonium reigned in the courtyard, when business was closed down till four, and the factors, all except the President, adjourned to the dining-hall. Our ancestors dined early, and dinner was a portentous affair. Padre Ovington, who, chaplain though he was, had evidently not learnt to abandon the pleasures of the table, describes it with evident gusto.[1] All the dishes were of pure silver, massy and

[1] *Op. cit.*, pp. 396–9.

THE INTERIOR OF THE OLD ENGLISH FACTORY

substantial, and so were the 'tosses' or cups.[1] Before dinner, a large silver ewer and basin for washing the hands was taken round by a *peon*. Indian, Portuguese, and English cooks were employed, so as to 'please the curiosity of every palate': *pulaos*, cabob curries with plenty of chutneys and relishes, and a 'dumpoked' fowl, that is a fowl stewed in butter and stuffed with almonds and raisins,[2] were ordinary dishes. This was washed down with plenty of 'generous Shiraz wine and arrack punch, served round the table'. On Sundays and holidays, the meal was made 'more large and splendid', with venison, peacocks, and other game, Persian fruits, such as apricots, plums, and cherries. European wines and bottled beer were added. The latter in particular excited the curiosity of the natives; a wealthy Indian who dined at the factory caused great amusement by asking how it was put in. When we hear that the meal sometimes ran to sixteen courses, we are able to understand the complaint that excessive indulgence in meat and alcohol was responsible for many deaths and much more sickness.[3] After dinner the silver ewer once again went round, and then the loyal toasts, the King, and the Company, were drunk by all.[4] Dinner over, all retired for the afternoon siesta. Work started again at four. At six the factory was cleared of outsiders and the gates were closed. Prayers were again read, after which supper was served. At supper the President often made his appearance; the meal was an informal one, and on sultry nights was often laid in the groves or gardens near the waterside, whither the factors repaired 'to spend an hour or two with a cold collation and a bottle of wine'. After supper, no one was allowed in or out, the porter having strict orders to that effect. To 'lie abroad' without the President's

[1] 'Toss' = Persian *ṭas*. Silver was cheaper than china or glass, hence the abundance of good plate at the Universities and other establishments of the seventeenth century.

[2] Persian *dampukhta*, stewed.

[3] 'Strong drink and flesh is mortal . . . this is the true cause our Bombay bills of mortality have swelled so high' (quoted in Anderson, *English in Western India*, p. 63).

[4] This was after the Restoration, of course. During the Commonwealth feeling was naturally against the monarchy. Charles II conciliated the Company by the gift of Bombay.

permission was a serious offence, involving a fine of forty shillings.

From this account it may be seen that the factory was 'more like unto a College, Monastery, or a house under Religious Orders than any other', as a contemporary writer puts it.[1] This was necessary for several reasons. The apprentices and younger writers were liable to many temptations in an Eastern town, from which it was imperative to preserve them. The dangers to which they were exposed may be gathered from Ovington's description of Bombay, where things were much laxer. There, 'Luxury, Immodesty and a prostitute dissolution of manners', together with 'a thousand other black infernal vices', combined with the climate, wrought fearful havoc, and gave rise to the saying that 'Two monsoons are the age of a man'.[2] Again, it was highly advisable to avoid brawls with the native population, and this offence was visited with peremptory chastisement. 'If any be drunk or abuse the natives they are to be set at the gate in irons all the day time, and all the night to be tied to the post in the house.'[3] Before the days of President Aungier, only a few privileged persons were allowed to bring their wives out, and the Company was, as we have seen already, determined to stop the English from forming *liaisons* with native women, and so falling into the degeneracy which overtook the Portuguese at Goa.[4] In a letter already quoted,[5] the factors write :—

'. . . taking Jentues [6] meets often with great trouble alsoe, tho' but very poor people having all of them husbands very early, who tho' they cohabit not, yet on such occasion apply to the Government where its never ended but with great charge and trouble. . . . It 's alsoe of very ill consequence that your Covenant Servants should intermarry with any of the people of the country or those of mixed race or *Mustechees*,[7] therefore we desire your Honour would continue it as a standing rule that none doe rise in your service, or rather bee not

[1] Sir Streynsham Master, quoted above.
[2] Ovington, p. 142.
[3] Sir Streynsham Master, quoted above.
[4] p. 18, *supra*.
[5] Yule, p. ccix, as above.
[6] *Gentoos*, a corruption of Portuguese *Gentio*, 'gentile' or heathen i.e. Hindus, as opposed to *Moros* or Muhammadans (Portuguese).
[7] *Mestico* (Portuguese), half-caste.

retained in your service as a Covenant Servant, as Factore or Merchant, that shall marry with any of the country not of Europe parents, but immediately be discharged from being either Factor, Merchant or higher quality. Writers if not to advance or sailors and soldiers of no higher quality than sergeant, may be permitted if your Honour shall think fitt as is amounge the Dutch, tho' among the Danes it is otherwise, they being all suplyed with Europe women.'

Ovington tells us of an experiment which was made in Bombay of bringing out girls from England as wives for the factors, but it was not, apparently, a great success.[1] The Company did its best to repress all 'disorderly and unchristian conversation', and to reduce all their people in their several factories and colonies, not only to a civil, but also to a religious and pious comportment, that may render our nation honorable, and the religion we profess amiable in the sight of those Heathens among whom they reside'.[2] Ovington publishes a resolution of the Company

'That the Agents and Chiefs, in their several factories, take care to prevent all profane swearing and taking the Name of God in vain by cursed oaths; all drunkenness and intemperance, all fornication and uncleanness; and that if any will not be reformed, and do not abstain from these vices, but after admonition and reprehension shall be found guilty again, that then such punishment shall be inflicted on them, consisting with the laws of God and this Kingdom, as the Agent and Council shall find their crime to deserve. And that if after such punishment inflicted, he or they will not amend or be reformed, then the Agent is strictly enjoined and required to send home for England by the next ships such person or persons so unreclaimable, that they may not remain in India, to the dishonour of God, the scandal of religion, the discredit of our Nation, and the perverting of others.'[3]

For the same purpose, the factory library was stocked with all manner of improving books. 'We have sent the works of that worthy servant of Christ, Mr. William Perkins, together with Foxe's Book of Martyrs, also Mr. Hakluyt's Voyages, to recreate their spirits with variety of history', writes the Company in 1611.[4] In 1686, Purchas's *Pilgrimes* was added, as

[1] *Op. cit.*, pp. 146–7.
[2] *Ibid.*, p. 406.
[3] *Op. cit.*, p. 407.
[4] *First Letter Book*, p. 419.

'very necessary for all men that would arrive at any maturity of understanding in the affairs of India and of the Dutch wiles, and former abuses of our Nation'. Sir George Oxinden complains of the lack of editions of the Fathers in the factory.[1]

An effort was made, not, we fear, very successfully, to reduce by the use of tea the mortality caused by excessive drinking. Among the Dutch, Ovington tells us, 'the teapot's seldom off the fire', but apparently the English factors, as in Mandelslo's days, preferred 'burnt wine', punch and arrack. Ovington waxes eloquent on the medicinal properties of tea. 'With some hot spices intermixt and boiled in the water', he says, 'tea has the repute of prevailing against the headache, gravel, and griping in the guts, and 'tis generally drunk in India, either with sugar-candy, or by the more curious, with small conserved lemons. The frequent use of this innocent tea, and the perpetual perspiration which is caused by the heat, which is augmented by this liquor, are the reason why the gout and the stone, agues, rheumatisms and catarrhs are rarely heard of in these parts.'[2]

After the Restoration, the feasts and fasts of the Church were strictly observed.

'Upon the great feasts of Christmas, Easter, and Whitsuntide we have the solemn service, public feasts, and no great business permitted to be done in the factory house, and all the Country people know why we are solemn, and feast, and are merry. So also for Gunpowder Treason day, and on the 29th of May for the King's birth and return. And upon the principal fasts we have very strict fasts kept, no business done in the house, and the public prayers used upon the occasion, as in Lent, especially upon Ash Wednesday, Good Friday, the 30th of January for the Martyrdom of King Charles the First, and some persons there are, of which the President is one, that keep weekly fasts upon every Friday. Tho' our fasts here are not as the Romanists and as our Church seems to direct, abstinence from flesh and eating of fish, but a mean diet, without distinction of

[1] In 1660, Mr. Rich sent by the *Eagle* to Surat a polyglot Bible. An Arabic translation of Grotius is also mentioned (Yule, *Hedges' Diary*, I. ccclii.

[2] See p. 107, *supra*.

meats; nay, generally none until night, but prayers and retirement.'[1]

These holidays were usually celebrated by expeditions into the country.

'The President', says Ovington, 'upon solemn days generally invites the whole factory abroad to some pleasant garden adjacent to the city, where they may sit shaded from the beams of the Sun, and refreshed by the neighbourhood of tanks and waterworks. The President and his Lady are brought hither in palanquins, supported each of them by six peons, which carry them by four at once on their shoulders. Before him at a little distance are carried two large flags or English Ensigns, with curious Persian or Arabian horses of state, which are of great value, rich in their trappings and gallantly equipped, that are led before him. The furniture of these and several other horses, whereon the factors ride, is very costly; the saddles are all of velvet richly embroidered, the headstalls, reins and croupers are all covered with solid wrought silver. The Captain of the Peons[2] at this time ascends his horse, and leads forty or fifty others with him, which attend the President on foot. Next the President follow the Council in large coaches, all open, except their wives are in them; the several knobs about them are all covered with silver, and they are drawn by a pair of stately oxen. After them succeed the rest of the factors, either in coaches or hackeries, or upon horses, which are kept by the Company to accommodate their President and people at these times, or whenever they fancy to take the air. In this pompous procession does the President, when he goes abroad, travel thro' the heart of the city.'[3]

The object of all this grandeur was to impress the natives, accustomed as they were to Mughal pomp and ceremony.

'This creates a respect from the natives as they pass along, strikes them with a regard to the English wherever they meet them; makes them value our friendship, and place and honour in our intimacy and acquaintance. The probity and grandeur of the English living hath formerly raised the Presidency of Surat to that veneration and esteem among the native inhabitants, that it has eclipsed the greatness of

[1] Sir Streynsham Master, quoted above.

[2] The *peons* played a prominent part in factory life, attending the factors on every occasion. Every morning and evening they went in a body to pay their *salaams* to the President. They were noted for their fidelity.

[3] *Op. cit.*, p. 398.

their own government, by encouraging the injured and distresed Indians to apply themselves for relief rather to our President than their Governor.' [1]

The Company had not forgotten the lesson which they had learnt from Roe, that if they wished to be respected, they must be mindful of their dignity. For this reason, too, even after death, the senior officials of the factory were treated with the utmost respect. Ovington speaks with admiration of the 'magnificent structures and stately monuments' in the European cemetery at Surat, 'whose large extent, beautiful architecture and aspiring heads make them visible at a remote distance, lovely objects of the sight, and give them the title of the principal ornaments and magnificencies about the city'.[2] These were obviously imitated from the tombs of the Mughal noblemen, and the most famous, with their 'stately towers and minarets', were those of President Breton, the Oxindens, and Aungier. Sir George Oxinden's funeral was a great function.

'The manner of our burying is so decent that the natives, (who are also very decent in that particular) though they may not come near a dead corpse by reason they esteem it a polluting or defiling themselves, nay to some it is pollution to see, hear or speak of a corpse, yet they will behold our burials, and at the funeral for Sir George Oxinden the streets, balconys and tops of the houses were so full as they could stand one by another. At the grave after the corpse is interred, there is money thrown and given to the poor people; and our burying place, which is large and spacious, is adorned with several great and many handsome tombs and monuments, which many of the great men of the country esteem worth their sight.' [3]

Here we must close our brief sketch of the daily life of the sturdy forerunners of the English in western India. In the hired house in Surat they laid, quite unconsciously, the foundation of a great Empire. Surat is now a shadow of its former glory. A busy native population still throngs the bazaars and the narrow streets with their carved wooden balconies. But the Tapti has silted up, and only small vessels

[1] Ovington, pp. 400–1. [2] *Op. cit.*, p. 405.
[3] Sir Streynsham Master, quoted above.

THE ENGLISH CEMETERY SURAT FROM THE SOUTH-EAST

THE ENGLISH CEMETERY SURAT FROM THE EAST

can ascend the river: the maritime trade has passed to Bombay, and Swally Road is deserted, save for occasional country craft. The Gopi Talao, where the President used to take the air in solemn state, has long since been drained. The mouldering castle walls frown silently upon the placid stream which was once the scene of so many gallant contests, and the pretentious tombs in the deserted graveyard are almost the only relics of the departed greatness of the place.

APPENDIX I

THE TOMBS IN THE ENGLISH CEMETERY AT SURAT

[The following details are mostly taken from a pamphlet by A. F. Bellasis, C.S., entitled *Old Tombs in the Cemeteries of Surat*, Education Society's Press, Byculla, 1868, being a reprint of an article by the author published in the *Journal of the Bombay Branch of the Royal Asiatic Society*, vi. 146. See also E. B. Eastwick, in Murray's *Bombay Handbook*, p. 317, and Murray, *Handbook, India, Burma, and Ceylon*, 1919.]

The tombs in the English cemetery at Surat are unique in many ways. Nothing quite like them is found in Calcutta or Madras. The idea of erecting these imposing structures over their dead was no doubt copied from the Mohammedans: the factors were familiar, for example, with the tombs at Sarkej near Ahmedabad. The Dutch in their turn tried to outrival their English neighbours; the gigantic sarcophagus of Governor Henry Adrian Van Reede (or Rheede), 1691, is an obvious attempt to eclipse the mausoleum of the Oxindens. Another idea was to impress the natives. To us, these cumbersome erections, with their mixture of Oriental and European architecture, seem quaint rather than imposing, but they were greatly admired in their day, and Ovington, Fryer, and other travellers in the seventeenth century refer to them with pride. They were evidently a show for sightseers, and were pointed out as standing monuments to the respectability and dignity of the Company's servants. They have suffered from vandalism and neglect; inscriptions have been removed, and the jovial Dutch commander's monument is no longer, as in Ovington's days, surmounted by 'three large punchbowls'.

The earliest and most graceful of the English tombs is the

pretty domed mausoleum of Francis Breton, with its quaint epitaph :

Viator (si saltem Christianus es) siste.
Siste inquam paululum, nec frustra erit,
Cum iacere hic scias Franciscum Bretonum,
Pro Honorabili Mercatorum Anglorum Societate
Mercaturam Orientalem Agentium Praesidem.
Qui
Cum per quinquennium
Summâ cum sedulitate et spectatâ integritate
Functus est officio suo, Vitâ functus est
Coelebs hinc migravit ad Nuptias Coelestes
Anno Christi MDC XL IX die XXI mensis Julij.

Satis est (Viator) te haec non nescire,
Lachrymam modo impende unam et abi.

Next in order comes the grand tomb of the Oxindens. 'Christopher', says Anderson, 'is commemorated by a cupola within the lofty and more expansive cupola raised in honour of his more distinguished brother, the President. The height of this monument is forty feet, the diameter twenty-five. Massive pillars support the cupolas, and round their interiors are galleries reached by a flight of many steps. The body of an Indian Viceroy might have found here a worthy resting-place : it is far too superb for the Chief of a factory, and his brother who was only a subordinate.'[1] The inscription runs as follows :

Hic situs est Christophorus Oxinden, probitatis
Exemplum vitâ, sed vitae morte caducae,
Intrat et exiit, hic incepta animamque finivit.
Ille dies tantum numerare Logista valebat,
Non annos, nam raptim exegit mors rationem.
Quaeritis, O Domini, quid damni vel quid habetis
Lucri ? vos servum, socium nos, perdidit ille
Vitam, sed per contra scribat mors mihi lucrum.
Exiit e vitâ Apr. 18. 1659.[2]

Sir George's epitaph, in the upper story, is more magniloquent :

Interrogas ? Amice Lector !
Quid sibi vult grandior haec structura ! Responsum habe,
In hoc gloriatur satis quod alteram illam grandem continet,
Superbit insuper quod una cum illâ tegit generosos duos fratres
Fraterrimos,
Qui et in vivis fuerunt et etiam in mortuis sunt quam coniunctissimi.
Alterum velis intelligas ? lege alibi.
Intelligas velis alterum ? lege hic.

[1] *English in Western India*, 1854, p. 92.
[2] The epitaph was written by Sir George. He came out to the East as a boy, hence his hexameters are not of the best !

Dominus Georgius Oxinden Cantianus
Filius natu tertius D. Iacobi Oxinden Equitis.
Ipse equestri dignitate ornatus
Anglorum in Indiâ, Persiâ, Arabiâ Praeses,
Insulae Bombayensis Gubernator
Ab illustri Societate pro qua presidebat et gubernabat
Ob maxima sua et repetita in eam merita
Singulari favoris et gratitudinis specimine honestatus.
Vir
Sanguinis splendore, rerum usu,
Fortitudine, prudentiâ, probitate,
Pereminentissimus
Cum plurimorum luctu, obiit Iulij 14°,
Cum plurimorum frequentiâ sepultus est Iulij 15°
Anno Domini 1669,
Anno Aetatis 50.
Heus Lector!
Ex magno hoc viro, vel mortuo aliquid proficias.

Another governor, Bartholomew Harris and his girl-wife, have a similar but less elaborate epitaph:

Hic iacent
Bartholemaeus Harris Armiger
Propugnaculi et insulae Bombayensis,
Nuper prefectus et pro Gubernatore Societate
Mercatorum Londinensium ad Indos
Orientales Negotiantium Suratiae Presidens,
Et Coniux sua Arabella
Ille Maij decimos
Anno { Aetatis XLV
Domini MDC XCIV }
Haec Martij vicis secundo
Anno { Aetatis XVIII
Domini MDC LXXXVI. }

'Annesley of Surat' has the following:

Hic iacet
Samuel Evance Annesley,
Honorabilis viri
Samuelis Annesley, Angli—
Et Susannae uxoris eius filius;
Natus Mart. 18 A.D. 1697–8.
Variolis correptus eodem die An: 1702.
Mortuus die 21.
Hic etiam iacet
Frater eius Caesar Annesley,
Natus 8vo Maij 1700.
Et morbo spasmi 30 Iulij Sequentis
Mortuus
Cum duobus abortivis.

A pathetic little monument is that of the young son of Henry Gary, 'qui hinc emigravit ad eternas mansiones, 19 August Anno 1658, anno aetatis 14'.

There are other tombs, ranging from 1708 to 1821. Many contain brief hints of forgotten tragedies ('Annesley, son of Lieut. Colonel Thomas Brownrigg, aged 2 months; and Margaret, his mother, who fell a victim for him'). John Blyth, infant, buried on October 3, 1773, has the following:

Happy the babe, who, privileged by fate
To shorter labour and to higher weight,
Received but yesterday the gift of breath,
Ordered to-morrow to return to Death.

Other tombs have no inscriptions, perhaps because, as Bellasis conjectures, they were removed by the natives to be used as curry-stones. A large structure, without any distinguishing mark, is supposed to be the resting-place of the great Gerald Aungier.[1] There is a graveyard at Swally, but it contains nothing of interest: it has already been pointed out that Tom Coryat probably lies in an unmarked sepulchre there.[2] Close to Swally, at the mouth of the Tapti, is the curious structure known as Vaux's tomb, which is a landmark to vessels crossing the bar. Vaux was a protégé of Sir Josia Child, and was Deputy Governor. He and his wife were drowned near the spot in 1697.

APPENDIX II

FORM OF A BILL OF ADVENTURE ISSUED BY THE EAST INDIA COMPANY

WHEREAS A.B. one of the Adventurers and one of the Bretheren of the Company of Merchants trading into the East Indies hath not only set down for his adventure with the said Company to the sum of £550 in their Fourth Voyage to the East Indies by the Cape Bonae Spei in the good ships called the *Ascension* and the *Union*, but hath also truly paid the said sum of £550 for his adventure:

WE THEREFORE, the Governor and Company, do, by this our present bill of Adventure, do promise and agree to and with the said A.B., that we, the said Governor and Company and our successors, shall and will, upon the return of the ships called the *Ascension* and *Union*, or either of them, set out by us in this present Fourth Voyage, or within convenient time after their said return in the same, deliver

[1] An inscription to this effect was added in 1916.
[2] See p. 90, *supra*.

to the said A.B. his executors, administrators or assignees a true and just account and payment of such stock, benefit and profit of stock as God shall send upon the said voyage, according to the general distribution, proportion, and allottment which shall be allotted, disposed and given to all and every the several adventurers, except and always reserved out of the said sum or stock before mentioned, for and to those of the right owners of the same, all such sums which shall in due time justly appear to the said Company to be adventured under the said A.B. by any underadventurer in the said Fourth Voyage, together with all the profit and benefit thereof without fraud or guile.—*First Letter Book*, p. 27 B.[1]

APPENDIX III

PAY BILLS OF THE SURAT FACTORY

(*a*) 1628–9.

Richard Wylde, President, £100.
John Skibbowe, £200.
Richard Boothbye, £100.
George Page, £100.
Arthur Suffild, Purser, £50.
John Willoughby, £50.
Nicholas Wooley, purser's Mate, £30.
Henry Glascocke, £50.
Ralph Rande, writer, £35.
Peter Mondaie, writer, £30.
Crispen Blagden, writer, £40.
Thomas Smith, writer, £25.
Clement Dunscombe, writer, £20.
Thomas Joice, £33⅓.
Robert Davison, steward, £20.
John Calf, writer, £20.
Thomas Wilborne (Mr. Wylde's man), £20.
George Turner (an unprofitable chirurgeon), £40.
John Blewe, Cook, £18.
William Wade, boy, ...
Two bakers, £36.

English Factories, 1624–9, p. 314.

[1] Cf. a later form of indenture in Ramsay Muir, *Making of British India*, pp. 87–8.

(*b*) 1649.

Francis Breton, President, £350.
Thos. Merry, £300 Member of Council.
Edward Pearce, £100 ,, ,, ,,
George Oxinden, £40 ,, ,, ,,
Andrew Baines, Minister, £50.
Anthony Clitherow, Warehouseman, £60
John Anthony, chirurgeon, £33.
Henry Young, £18.
John Adler, £18.
Nicholas Buckeridge, £25.
Walter Gollofer, £25.
John Broadbent, £20.
Edward Locke, chirurgeon's mate, £22 4*s*.
John Chambers, 'boarder' . . . .
William Noke, President's servant, £4 16*s*.
George Pepys, Mr. Merry's servant, £9.
Herman Hill, trumpeter, £24.
John Wilson, cook, £14 18*s*.

English Factories, 1646–50, p. 271.

APPENDIX IV

SEPARATE VOYAGES OF THE EAST INDIA COMPANY, 1601–12

Voyage.	*Fleet.*	*Captain.*	*Capital.* £	*Profit per cent.*	*Remarks.*
1st voyage, 1601	*Dragon, Hector, Ascension, Susan*, and *Gift*	James Lancaster	68,373	95	Sailed April 22, 1601; Achin, June 5, 1602; Bantam; returned Sept. 11, 1603.
2nd voyage, 1604	*Dragon, Hector, Ascension, Susan*	H. Middleton	60,450	95	Bantam and Amboyna. *Susan* lost.
3rd voyage, 1607	*Dragon, Hector, Consent*	Keeling.	53,500	234	Left the *Hector* with Captain William Hawkins at Socotia to go on to Surat. Hawkins establishes Surat Factory and remainder go to Bantam and Amboyna.
4th voyage, 1608	*Ascension* and *Union*	Sharpeigh	33,000	—	Discover Aden and Seychelles. *Ascension* wrecked in Gulf of Cambay; Jourdain lands. *Union* goes to Achin, and is wrecked off Brittany on homeward voyage.
5th voyage, 1609	*Consent*	David Middleton	13,900	234	
6th voyage, 1610	*Trades Increase, Peppercorne, Darling*	Henry Middleton	82,000	121	Middleton's adventures in the Red Sea: he takes off Hawkins and Jourdain at Surat; loses *Trades Increase* off Bantam, and dies; Downton returns with *Peppercorne* Nov. 19, 1613.
7th voyage, 1611	*Globe*	Anthony Hippon	71,581 (7th and 8th voyages)	218	Saris reaches Japan, finds William Adams at Firando and establishes a factory there (1613).
8th voyage, 1611	*Clove, Hector, Thomas*	John Saris			
9th voyage, 1612	*James*	Edward Marlowe	76,375 (9th, 10th and 11th voyages)	211	
10th voyage, 1612	*Hosiander, Solomon, Red Dragon*	Best			Sea-fight at Swally Nov. 29—Dec. 24, 1612. Best defeats the Portuguese.
11th voyage, 1612	*Solomon*	Best			
12th voyage, 1613	*Expedition*	Christopher Newport	7,200	160	Takes Shirley, King of Persia's ambassador, to Jask.

(For the materials for this list, see Hunter, *History of British India*, i. 290–2, and authorities there quoted. The older books group together the 7th and 8th, and the 9th, 10th, and 11th voyages, which were really 'Joint Stocks'. It is necessary, however, to keep them separate, as these are the numbers referred to by Purchas.)

APPENDIX V

THÉVENOT'S ACCOUNT OF SURAT

[Jean de Thévenot, 1633–67, travelled in the Levant, Asia Minor, and Persia 1655–65. He sailed in the *Hopewell*, November 1665, from Basra, reaching Surat January 10, 1666. He stayed in India one year, journeyed from Surat to Masulipatam via Golconda and back, and died on his way home, November 28, 1667. The following selections from his *Voyages aux Indes Orientales*[1] (3rd ed., 12mo, Amsterdam, 1727) are an excellent commentary on the English accounts of Surat.]

i. The Town of Surat (Chapter VII, p. 44)

La ville de Sourat est située au vingtuniéme degré et quelques minutes de latitude et est arrosée de la rivière de Tapty. Quand j'y arrivai, ses murailles n'étoient que de terre et presque toutes ruinées : mais on commençoit à en bâtir de brique : on les faisoit épaisses d'une toise et demie : on ne leur donnoit que la même hauteur et cependant on avoit dessein de fortifier cette place autant que l'on pourroit, à cause de l'irruption qu'un Raja,[2] dont je parlerai dans la suite, y avoit faite quelque tems auparavant ; cependant l'Ingenieur a fait une faute considerable aux alignmens de ses murs : il les a batis si près de la Forteresse, que dans la Ville on sera à couvert de l'artillerie du Château, et on pourra aisément incommoder du mousquet ceux qui le dessendront.

Ces nouvelles murailles rendent la Ville bien plus petite qu'elle n'étoit auparavant ; car on n'y enferme point quantité de maisons faites de cannes, qui ci-devant étoient dans son enceinte, et dont plusiers gens qui y ont intrêt en prétendent un grand dédommagement. Sourat est de mediocre grandeur, et il est difficile de dire au juste le nombre de ses Habitans, parce que les saisons le rendent inégal : il y en a toûjours beaucoup toute l'année ; mais au tems de la Monson, c'est à dire au tems que les Vaisseaux peuvent aller et venir aux Indes sans danger, aux mois de Novembre, Decembre, Janvier, Février et Mars, et même en Avril, la ville est si

[1] The full title is : *Les Voyages de M. de Thévenot aux Indes Orientales, contenant La Relation de l'Indoustan*, troisième édition, à Amsterdam chez Michel Charles le Céne, MDCCXXVII, livre premier.

[2] Sivaji.

pleine de monde, que l'on a de la peine à se loger commodément, et ses trois Faux Bourgs en sont remplis. . . .

(p. 46.) After describing the various inhabitants, Moors, Gentiles, and Parsis, he goes on :

Il y a des gens extrêmement riches à Sourat, et un Banian qui est de mes amis, appellé Vargivosa, est estimé avoir au moins huit millions de bien. Les Anglois et les Hollandois y ont leurs Maisons, qu'on nomme Loges et Comptoirs : Elles ont de fort beaux apartemens, et les Anglois y ont établi le bureau general de leur Commerce. Il y a bien cent Maisons Catholiques à Sourat.

Son Château est bâti sur le bord de la Riviere, à l'extrémité de la Ville, du côté de Midi, pour en defendre l'entrée à ceux qui voudroient l'attaquer, en remontant le Tapty. Cette Fortresse est d'une grandeur raisonnable : elle est quarrée et flanquée à chaque coin d'une grosse Tour. Ses fossez sont remplis de l'eau de la Mer par trois côtez, et elle est arrosée de la rivière au quatriéme, qui est au Couchant. On y voit paroître plusiers piéces de canon par les embrazures : on y garde les revenues du Roi, qui se tirent de la Province, et on ne les lui envoie jamais sans un ordre exprès : On y entre du couchant par une belle porte qui est dans le Bazar ou Meïdan : le Bureau du Fermier de la Doüane est auprès, et ce Château a son Gouverneur particulier, comme la Ville le sien.

Les Maisons de cette Ville, pour lesquelles on a voulu faire de la dépense sont plates comme en Perse et assez bien baties ; mais elles coûtent cher, parce qu'il n'y a point de pierre dans le Pais : comme on est obligé à se servir de brique et de chaux, il y entre beaucoup de bois de charpente qu'il faut apporter de Daman par Mer, celui du Païs qu'on prend fort loin étant beaucoup plus cher à cause qu'il le faut voiturer par terre. . . .

(p. 49.) Les ruës de Sourat sont larges et unies, mais elles ne sont point pavées. . . . Les Chrétiens et les Mahometans y mangent d'ordinaire de la chair de la vache, tant parce qu'elle y est meillure que celle de bœuf, qu'à cause que les bœufs servent à labourer la terre et à transporter tous les fardeaux. Le mouton qu'on y mange est assez bon : mais on a outre cela, des poules, des poulets, des pigeons, du cochon et de toute sorte de chasse.

ii. The Port of Surat (Chapter XV)

La Barre de Sourat où les vaisseaux arrivent presentement, n'en est pas le vrai port : on ne peut l'appeler au plus qu'une rade : et ce n'est pas sans raison que j'ai dit au commencement de ce livre, qu'à cause des Sables qui empêchent les vaisseaux de passer outre, on l'appelle la Barre. Effectivement il y en a si peu des fonds, qu'encore que les vaisseaux soient déchargés, les marées ordinaires ne suffisent pas pour les faire avancer, et on est obligé d'attendre celle de la pleine lune ; mais alors ils vont jusques devant Sourat, particulierement quand ils ont besoin de radoube. Les petites barques viennent aisément devant la Ville pour peu qu'il ait de marée.

Le vrai Port de Sourat est Sonaly à deux lieues de la Barre. Il n'est éloigné de la Ville que de quatre lieues et demie, et on passe la riviere devant la Ville pour y aller par terre. Tous les Vaisseaux mouilloient autrefois à ce Port où il y a bon ancrage ; mais parce que la Douane y étoit souvent fraudée, on a défendu d'y venir et personne n'y est allé depuis l'année mil six cents soixante, excepté les Anglois et les Hollandois, à qui on permet toujours d'y ancrer, et qui y ont chacun leur magazin. Ce Port leur donne une belle commodité pour sauver ce qu'ils veulent sans payer de droits ; et les carrosses des Gouverneurs, Commandeurs ou Presidens de ces deux Nations, qui se promenent souvent en ces quartiers-là, pourroient aisément enlever tout ce qui seroit en petit volume dans leurs Vaisseaux. Ils ont même des Jardins à Sonaly, sur le bord de la mer, et chacun un petit port où ils mettent leurs bots ou barques : si bien qu'il ne tient qu'à eux de ne pas païer la Doüane de beaucoup de choses.

Depuis que la défense a été faite aux autres Nations de mouiller à Sonaly, il y a toûjours un grand abord de Vaisseaux à la Barre, quoi qu'ils y soient fort incommodez : car aucun des Vaisseaux de la Perse, de l'Arabie heureuse, ni generalement de tous les Païs des Indes, n'a cessé d'y venir ; et ainsi la défense d'aborder à Sonaly n'a rien diminué du profit de la Doüane, qui rend toûjours au Roi chaque année douze leks de roupies, chaque lek valant cent mille livres ou environ. Le Doüanier est More, et c'est du Gouverneur de Sourat qu'il tient sa commission. Les Commis sont Banians, le reste des gens de la Douane, comme Gardes, Porte-faix et autres sont aussi Mores, et on les appelle les Pions de la Douane.

iii. The Governors of Surat (Chapter X)

Il y a deux Gouverneurs ou Nababs à Sourat qui ne sont dans aucune dépendance l'un de l'autre et ne rendent pas raison de leurs actions qu'au Roi. L'un commande au Château, et l'autre à la ville ; et ils n'entreprennent point sur les droits ou fonctions l'un de l'autre.

iv. *The Peons* (Chapter I)

Cependant il y en a sur le bord de la rivière grand nombre de *Pions*, qui sont des valets qu'on emploie à toute sorte de service et qu'on loue par jour si l'on veut, comme l'on fait les Estafiers en Italie. Ces Pions de la douanne ont en main de grosses cannes pour faire retirer le peuple afin que ceux que l'on débarque ne puissent avoir aucune communication avec personne : et pour plus grande seureté ils se tiennent en paye des deux côtés du passage.

v. *The Rapacity of the Customs Officers* (*ibid.*)

Il faut ôter le bonnet ou turban, la ceinture, les souliers, les chausses et le reste des habits, s'il plait aux visiteurs. Il n'y a pas un seul endroit du corps où ils ne portent pas la main. . . . On me fit d'abord reconnoître ce qui m'appartenoit, et mes valises aiant été apportées au milieu de la sale, elles furent ouvertes et vuidées. Chaque pièce fut examinée l'une après l'autre : quoique je n'eusse aucune merchandise on fouilla partout ; mon matelas fut entièrement decousu, on décola le pommeau d'un de mes pistolets, on passa des brochettes dans les étuis ; et enfin après que les Commis se furent satisfaits de la vûë de mes hardes, on me congedia, et j'en fus quitte pour la Douane de mon argent. Ce ne fut pas peu de bonheur pour moi d'être sitôt dépêché ; car il y a des gens qui attendent quelque fois un mois de tems avant que pouvoir retirer leurs hardes, et principalement ceux qui ont des marchandises, pour lesquelles ils paient à cette Douane quatre per cent si ce sont des Chrétiens, et cinq per cent si ce sont des Banians.

vi. *The Tombs of the Factors* (Chapter XIII)

Les cimetieres de Sourat sont hors la ville à trois ou quatre cents pas de la Porte Baroche. Les Catholiques y ont le leur en particulier. Les Anglois et les Hollandois y ont aussi le leur, ainsi que quelques religieux Indiens. Les Anglois et les Hollandois afectent d'orner leurs Sepultures de pyramides de brique, revêtües de chaux ; et comme j'y étois, on en batissoit une pour un Commandeur Hollandois, qui devoit coûter huit mille francs. Il y a une entr'autres d'un certain beuveur qui avoit été relegué dans les Indes par les Etats Generaux, et qu'on disoit être parent du Prince d'Orange : on lui a élevé un monument comme aux autres gens de marque : mais pour faire connoître qu'il savoit bien boire, l'on a mis une grande tasse de pierre, et une au bas à chaque coin du Tombeau, et auprès de chaque tasse il y a la figure d'un pain de sucre ; et quand les Hollandois vont se divertir auprès de cette sepulture, ils font cent ragouts dans ces tasses, et se servent d'autres plus petites tasses pour tirer ce qu'ils ont apprêté dans ces grands, afin de boire ou de manger.

INDEX